Achievement and Inclusion in Schools

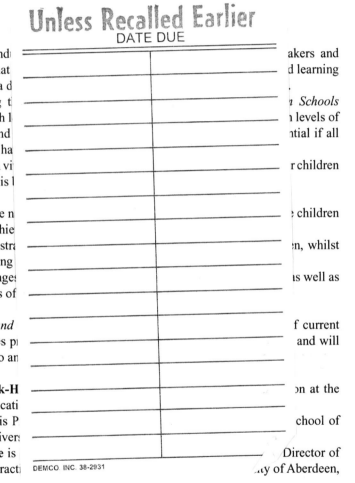

There is an end   akers and
practitioners that   d learning
difficult, have a d

  Challenging t   *Schools*
argues that high l   *levels of*
achievement and   *ntial if all*
children are to ha

  Packed with vi   r children
and schools, this l

- What is the n   children
  and the achie
- Are there str   n, whilst
  safeguarding
- What change   is well as
  high levels of

Achievement and   f current
issues, provides p   and will
be of interest to an

Kristine Black-H   on at the
Faculty of Educati
Lani Florian is P   chool of
Education, Univers
Martyn Rouse is   Director of
the Inclusive Pract   .ty of Aberdeen,
Scotland.

Achievement and Inclusion in Schools

Kristine Black-Hawkins, Lani Florian and Martyn Rouse

Routledge
Taylor & Francis Group

LONDON AND NEW YORK

First published 2007
by Routledge
2 Park Square, Milton Park, Abingdon, Oxon OX14 4RN

Simultaneously published in the USA and Canada
by Routledge
270 Madison Ave, New York, NY 10016

Transferred to Digital Printing 2008

Routledge is an imprint of the Taylor & Francis Group, an informa business

© 2007 Kristine Black-Hawkins, Lani Florian and Martyn Rouse

Typeset in Times by
HWA Text and Data Management, Tunbridge Wells
Printed and bound in Great Britain by
TJI Digital, Padstow, Cornwall

British Library Cataloguing in Publication Data
A catalogue record for this book is available from the British Library

Library of Congress Cataloging-in-Publication Data
A catalog record for this book has been requested

ISBN10: 0–415–39197–0 (hbk)
ISBN10: 0–415–39198–9 (pbk)
ISBN10: 0–203–94522–0 (ebk)

ISBN13: 978–0–415–39197–9 (hbk)
ISBN13: 978–0–415–39198–6 (pbk)
ISBN13: 978–0–203–94522–3 (ebk)

Contents

List of boxes and tables   vii
Acknowledgements   ix

1 Thinking about achievement, inclusion and the use of evidence   1

PART I
The nature of achievement and inclusion in schools   **13**

2 Understanding the relationship between inclusion and
   achievement   15

3 National datasets: what do they tell us about achievement
   and inclusion?   32

4 Examining the relationship between inclusion and achievement:
   the *Framework for Participation*   45

PART II
The case studies   **55**

5 Kingsley Primary School   59

6 Amadeus Primary School   72

7 Harbour Community School   86

8 Chester Community School   101

PART III
Learning from others: learning from ourselves   **117**

9 Learning from others: achievement and inclusion across
   the case study schools   119

10 Researching achievement and inclusion in your school   135

   References   154
   Index   159

Boxes and tables

Boxes

1.1	Thinking about achievement	3
1.2	Thinking about inclusion	4
1.3	Thinking about the use of research evidence	5
1.4	The relationship between achievement, inclusion and evidence	6
2.1	Summary of governmental usage of inclusion	20
2.2	Being healthy	26
2.3	Extract from Ofsted SEF	27
3.1	Categories of special educational needs	36
4.1	Principal elements of participation	47
4.2	The *Framework for Participation* sets out to…	50
4.3	Sections of the *Framework for Participation*	51
4.4	'Who?', 'What?' and 'Why?' of participation	51
4.5	Elements and questions of the *Framework for Participation*	52
10.1	Examining understandings of achievement in a school	138
10.2	Examining understandings of inclusion in a school	138
10.3	Examining understandings of the relationship between achievement and inclusion in a school	139
10.4	Paying attention to the nature of the research evidence	141
10.5	Existing knowledge, knowing and not knowing	142
10.6	Considering the ethics of learning from others when researching achievement and inclusion	144
10.7	Sections and their elements in the *Framework for Participation*	148
10.8	Evidence to support the *Framework for Participation*	149

Tables

II.1	Snapshot of LA Key Stage scores for 2005	57
5.1	Key Stage 2 results 2000 and 2003	69
5.2	Improvement measure for Key Stage 2 SATs, 2000–3	69
6.1	KS2 English test results, 2001–5	84
6.2	KS2 Mathematics test results, 2001–5	84

6.3   KS2 Science test results, 2001–5   84
6.4   Improvement measure for KS2 test, 2001–5   84
6.5   Children in Year 6 at Amadeus Primary School   84
7.1   Percentages of Year 11 students on selected variables in Harbour
      School and the LA, 2004   86
7.2   Mean achievement statistics for Harbour School and the whole
      LA, 2003   93
7.3   Harbour School and three comparison schools in the LA with
      lower percentage of students identified as having SEN, 2005   94
7.4   Value-added measures 2005   100
8.1   Percentages of Year 11 students on selected variables in Chester
      School and the LA, 2004   113
8.2   Chester School and three comparison schools with lower
      percentages of students identified as having SEN, 2005   114
8.3   Mean 2003 Year 11 achievement statistics for Chester School
      and the LA   114
8.4   Value-added, 2005   114

Acknowledgements

The research reported in this book would not have been possible without the generosity of the staff, children and young people in the four case study schools that are at the heart of this book. We hope that their willingness to allow us into their busy schools, to take time to talk with us, and to permit us to observe is rewarded with the satisfaction of knowing that what they have shared helps us all to deepen our understanding of inclusive practice. Thanks are also due to the local authority colleagues who worked closely with us to identify the case study schools.

Colleagues in Cambridge have provided intellectual stimulation and critical friendship. Stephen Jull worked with us as a research associate, collecting data and participating in the data analysis during a busy year while he was also as a doctoral student. We are grateful for financial support from the Wallenberg Research Centre and the Research and Development Fund in the Faculty of Education at the University of Cambridge. Special thanks are due to our wonderful secretary, Lyndsay Upex, for the hours she spent helping to prepare the manuscript.

Finally, we are indebted to Alison Foyle and her colleagues at Routledge for encouraging us to write the book and then patiently waiting for the final manuscript.

1 Thinking about achievement, inclusion and the use of evidence

Understanding the purposes of schools and their role in society challenges all who are engaged in education, whether they work in schools, universities or national or local government. Certain dilemmas seem to occur more often than others, perhaps because they are particularly important to current educational debates, but also because they are especially problematic so that straightforward solutions are unlikely and unhelpful. This book sets out to address three such contemporary concerns and to explore the relationship between them. These are: (i) the concept of achievement, (ii) meanings of inclusion and (iii) the use of evidence to inform educational policies and practices. We have chosen these themes because of our observation that some schools continue to resist pressures to become more inclusive because they are concerned that doing so will have a negative effect on the academic achievement of their students and/or lower overall standards. This book presents a critical examination of available evidence and offers guidance to those who wish to undertake research on this complex topic.

Primarily, this book is about the inclusion and the achievement of children and young people in education. In particular, we consider the challenges of raising the achievement of all students, whilst safeguarding the inclusion of those few who are more vulnerable to processes of exclusion from mainstream schools. A central argument, throughout the book, is that high levels of inclusion can be entirely compatible with high levels of achievement and, furthermore, that combining the two is not only possible but essential if all children are to have the opportunity to participate fully in education. However, we also recognise that doing so can make great demands on those who work in classrooms and schools.

The book is also about the nature of knowledge and research and what counts as evidence. We provide a critique of methods typically used to examine inclusion and achievement and then present, in more detail, our own approach to such research, using mixed methods that contrast with but complement each other. In so doing we consider the implications for different levels of interest and concern: whether focusing on an individual child, an identified group of children, a classroom, a whole school or across a local authority. We then offer practical research guidance for those who wish to identify strategies, within their own working contexts, to raise the achievement and inclusion of all.

At the heart of the book, however, are stories from four schools, which relate the everyday experiences of children, young people and practitioners. Each school has set out to be as inclusive as possible whilst also aiming to raise the achievements of all its students. How this is undertaken, as well as the successes accomplished and challenges encountered, varies from school to school. The stories thus provide an illustrative framework for the reader to question, research and understand their own policies and practices at whatever level.

Questioning inclusion, achievement and evidence

Boxes 1.1–1.3 provide sets of questions around the three key concerns of the book. The intention of these questions is to begin a debate around different understandings of achievement, inclusion and evidence, both conceptually and in practice. Box 1.4 offers additional questions, intended to inform discussions about the *relationship* between these three different sets of questions. Together they offer an introduction to the discussion which follows in this chapter and which is continued throughout the book.

Education for all? A perspective from England

In this part of the chapter we introduce some contextual background to achievement and inclusion by placing these ideas in a broader educational, social and historical framework. We present a more detailed examination of current definitions and interpretations in the following two chapters. We have used the term 'education for all?' as a motif here because it represents an aspiration which seems to be universally accepted and yet in practice is fraught with complications. In 1948 the United Nations Declaration of Universal Human Rights identified education as a fundamental right for all children. However, even now interpretations of both 'education' and 'all children' vary across countries and time.

In countries with long histories of compulsory school attendance, 'education for all' raises an important set of questions. These relate to which children and young people have the right to receive which forms of education. That is: who is to be included where, and how might this support their achievements? And, who is to be excluded from where, and how might this limit their achievements? In England, the options are many: between state and private schools, mainstream and special, one local school or another, one type of special school or another, selective entry or comprehensive, single sex or mixed, faith or not, specialist status (which specialism?) or not, 'leading edge' or 'in special measures', and so forth. Once a child is placed in a school, further selections are made: for example, being placed in a particular ability group in a primary class or a particular 'set' in a secondary school, or the use of small group withdrawal work or in-class support. Finally, other policies and practices that result in the temporary and permanent exclusion of children and young people also have a profound impact on the achievement of 'education for all'.

Box 1.1 Thinking about achievement

- What counts as educational achievement?
  - academic?
  - social?
  - emotional?
  - creative?
  - physical?
- Are some types of achievement more highly valued than others?
  - If so which ones?
  - Why?
  - And, by whom?
- How is achievement assessed and recorded?
  - What are the purposes of assessment?
  - Who are its audiences?
- To what extent does achievement involve making comparisons with:
  - other students (ranking)?
  - standardised norms (often expressed as a quotient)?
  - pre-specified criteria (as in national curriculum levels and targets)?
  - chronological age (as in, 'he is two years behind his age')?
  - previous attainment (personally referenced or ipsative assessment)?
- What is the relationship between achievement and …
  - ability?
  - aptitude?
  - attainment?
  - performance?
  - standards?
  - progress?
- How far are the achievements of children and young people influenced by factors that are:
  - within individual students?
  - in classrooms, including the role of practitioners?
  - institutional (across whole schools)?
  - within families and local communities?
  - national (socially, politically, culturally)?

Despite a policy of compulsory school attendance, historically, in England, education has been seen by some people not so much as a right to be enjoyed by all, but more of a privilege for those considered most likely to benefit from it. The extent of this view is important to bear in mind when considering issues of 'education for all', particularly in countries that have been influenced by or have inherited the English education system. A fundamental structural problem of equal opportunity lies at the heart of a system where those considered capable of high

Box 1.2   Thinking about inclusion

- What counts as educational inclusion?
- What kinds of opportunities and experiences are important to children and young people?
- Is the inclusion of some children and young people more/less highly valued (acceptable/unacceptable) than others?
  - If so, who?
  - Why?
  - And, by whom?
- How is inclusion assessed and recorded?
  - For what purposes?
  - Who are its audience?
- What is the relationship between inclusion and ...
  - exclusion?
  - integration?
  - participation?
  - the identification of special educational needs?
  - different kinds of special educational needs and disability?
- How far is the inclusion of children and young people influenced by factors that are:
  - within individual students?
  - in classrooms, including the role of practitioners?
  - institutional (across whole schools)?
  - within families and local communities?
  - national (socially, politically, culturally)?

achievements are encouraged to stay at school and beyond into higher education, whilst those who struggle, because their learning needs are not properly addressed, or their parents are not able to advocate for their interests, may be marginalised in school or leave education at the earliest opportunity. Thus, in many cases, the more successful the student, the greater the educational opportunities he or she is given, and the less successful the student, the fewer he or she is allowed.

Educational achievement for all?

A brief look at the history of publicly funded English schools provides ample evidence of this tension between three ways of conceptualising provision. These are: (i) some education for *all*, (ii) more education for *some* and (iii) different education for *others*. These variations in the amount, quality and nature of provision are not only formed by educational considerations, they are also fundamentally influenced by political and ideological stances. Decisions about who gets what have been largely determined by a series of testing and assessment procedures,

Box 1.3   Thinking about the use of research evidence

- What counts as research evidence?
- Are some forms of evidence more highly valued than others?
  - If so, what ones?
  - Why?
  - And, by whom?
- How do we gather, select and record evidence?
  - What are the purposes of doing so?
  - Who are its audiences?
- What is the nature of evidence based on ...
  - practitioner knowledge and experience?
  - practitioner research?
  - students' perspectives?
  - 'academic' research?
  - large-scale national data sets?
  - Government publications, advice and legislation?
- What is the influence of research evidence on:
  - the experiences of individual children and young people?
  - the experiences of identified groups of students?
  - the experiences of students and practitioners in classrooms?
  - policies and practices in institutions (across whole schools)?
  - local decision making?
  - national decision making?

intended to categorise, select and group students based on notions of similarities and differences. Perhaps the most profound of these, in terms of its enduring influence, has been the 1944 Butler Education Act. This introduced national IQ tests for children at age 11, so as to allocate them either to a grammar or a secondary modern school (and, in a few areas, a third option of technical schools). This process was based on three core beliefs. First, that a child's intelligence, or intellect, is a fixed entity unlikely to develop over time. Second, that assessing a person's intelligence can be easily and accurately accomplished. Third, that children can be categorised into two (or possibly three) 'types' of learners and that they will learn best in classes and schools which reflect these differences.

However, during the 1960s there was growing concern that this selection process ignored the educational needs of the vast majority of children who were placed in secondary modern schools. (Approximately 80 per cent of children attended secondary modern schools, although actual figures varied across the country.) Many secondary modern schools, when compared to the grammar schools, were poorly staffed and under-funded, with low expectations of both staff and students. Furthermore, until the school leaving age was raised in 1972, the majority of young people left secondary modern schools at age 15 with no

Box 1.4   The relationship between achievement, inclusion and evidence

- What might be the effects of greater inclusion on the achievement:
  - of individual children and young people?
  - of identified groups of students?
  - in classrooms?
  - institutionally (across whole schools)?
  - locally?
  - nationally?
- What might be the effects of raising achievement on the inclusion:
  - of individual children and young people?
  - of identified groups of students?
  - in classrooms?
  - institutionally (across whole schools)?
  - locally?
  - nationally?
- In what ways do assumptions about the 'normal distribution' of ability and attainment influence thinking and practice relating to inclusion and achievement?
- What changes can a school make to raise the achievement of all children and young people, whilst safeguarding the inclusion of others who are more vulnerable?
- What different kinds of research evidence are needed to address these questions, plus:
  - strengths and limitations of different ways of monitoring achievement?
  - strengths and limitations of different of ways of monitoring inclusion?

nationally recognised qualifications. Meanwhile, grammar school students often stayed in school until they were aged 18, when they had the chance to take Advanced Level examinations. A Levels then, as now, provided access to university places and/or professional training. Thus, not only were a child's future educational achievements largely determined by the age of 11, so were the types of employment and social and economic opportunities allowed them as adults. The post-war vision of an inclusive 'secondary education for all' was something of an illusion.

These inequities in the system led to the government's decision to introduce a non-selective comprehensive secondary school system, intended to provide greater equality of opportunity for all. However, whilst some progress has been made throughout the decades of comprehensive reorganisation in England, provision remains patchy and selective grammar schools continue to exist in about 25 per cent of local authorities. Further, there are those (for example Marks, 2000) who argue for the reintroduction of grammar schools on a national scale as a way of improving standards. Such critics believe that doing so will allow a return to the quasi-meritocratic era of the past in which some working-class children were able to 'escape' from their circumstances. And, even in comprehensive schools, it was not until 1988 that the two systems of public examinations for 'academic' and 'non-academic' students were abolished, and most students were examined through the General Certificate of Secondary Education (GCSE).

Progress towards a more comprehensive educational system was slow, in part, because all schools have their histories and traditions and most importantly they serve particular communities. Thus even non-selective comprehensive schools, in relatively close proximity to one another, may offer very different experiences to their students. This has been exacerbated, particularly since the 1990s, by the commitment of both Conservative and Labour governments to the values of competition and parental choice in education (see, for example, DfEE, 1992, *Choice and Diversity*). However, competition results in winners and losers. As Whitty (1997) notes, if some schools are considered to be succeeding, others must be relatively failing, which is unlikely to promote the educational achievements of children and young people who attend the latter. And, as Thrupp and Tomlinson (2005: 551) argue, 'choice' is a misnomer when it becomes an option 'reserved for privileged choosers', so that 'a good education is a prize to be competitively sought, not a democratic right for every child'.

Apple (2006) notes that once certain local schools are considered to be particularly successful they are able to exert their own covert selection processes, because the focus moves away 'from what the school does for the student to what the student does for the school' (p.59). In terms of a marketplace metaphor, demand for places in the most popular schools invariably outstrips supply and so such schools are able to make choices about which children and parents are likely to enhance their future position in local league tables.

Certainly, there can be huge variations in students' academic attainments amongst groups of local schools, both at primary and at secondary levels (see, for example, the DfES performance tables). For the latter, these disparities might be seen to echo past differences between grammars and secondary moderns. Harris and Ranson (2005: 575) suggest that choice, as exercised by middle-class parents, has led to the 'homogenisation of the social composition' of schools and this has strengthened further 'the stubborn relationship between social disadvantage and underachievement' in education (p.584). The sharp increase in the number of 'specialist' schools at secondary level (see DfEE, 2001, and DfES, 2005a), and opportunities for schools to select a proportion of their students according to particular aptitudes, has further intensified differences between schools in terms of student intake.

Educational inclusion for all?

Until 1970, educational inclusion could never be a realisable goal in England, since it was not until the Education Act of that year that all children and young people finally had the right to attend school. Prior to this, some children were assessed as being 'ineducable' and so no state educational provision was made for them. From 1970, such children were categorised as being 'severely educationally sub-normal' (subsequently, 'severe learning difficulties') and were to attend schools specially established for them. This change in English education legislation extended segregated provision, which had already been made for other identified groups of children and young people; for example, there had been special schools for children with physical or sensory disabilities for a century or more. Indeed, this belief in the need for two separate forms of schooling – one for children who are considered to be 'ordinary' and another for those who are not – has been part of the English education system since the introduction of compulsory schooling. As the Royal Commission for the Blind, Deaf and Dumb reported in 1889: 'There are a great many backward children in our elementary schools who require a different treatment to that of the ordinary children' (p.104; cited in Copeland, 2003: 45).

Therefore, whilst the 1970 Act finally gave all children the right to be educated in a school, the existence of a segregated (special) system was increasingly being seen, by some, as a way of perpetuating the exclusion of vulnerable children from the mainstream entitlements allowed to others. As Florian (2007: 7) notes:

> Advocates and critics have simultaneously hailed and condemned [special education] as both a means of achieving equal educational opportunities and a perpetuator of injustice in education.

So, is the primary purpose of special schools to protect the educational rights of the most vulnerable children by providing suitable learning experiences in appropriate settings? Or, are they intended to protect the educational rights of the majority of children in mainstream schools, so that their learning is not disrupted by the presence of children whose identified special educational needs are considered to be especially demanding? The answers to these questions are not straightforward but may well be partly determined by the particular viewpoint of any respondent, whether as a student, a parent, a teacher or whoever.

This brief overview of the development of English schooling indicates a complex terrain in which current attempts to promote inclusive practice, widen participation and raise achievement are strongly influenced, some would say constrained, by a series of largely unquestioned assumptions. These are concerned with the presumed differences between children, historical patterns of provision and forms of institutional inertia which make fundamental change difficult, but not impossible.

Inclusion, accountability and standards

Inclusion in education is both the means for, and a consequence of, school systems attempting to address issues of inequality by widening access and participation. In parallel with this move to greater inclusion, the past two decades have seen a preoccupation in many countries with greater accountability and raising standards. Governments throughout the world have enacted what are known as 'standards-based reforms' to improve national competitiveness and the efficiency of their school systems. A common intention of many of these policies has been to close the achievement gap between the highest performing students and those who do not perform so well. And yet, those students, who have been identified as having special educational needs, have not been a central feature of the first wave of these reforms.

It is only recently that their achievements have also been scrutinised as it has been realised that special education provision is not only often very expensive, but is also a means by which schools that are under pressure to raise standards might 'hide' their lowest achieving students (Rouse and McLaughlin, 2007). Therefore, debates about inclusion now involve considerations of how all children and young people might be meaningfully included in national curricula and systems of assessment and how their participation might be judged. In a culture in which schools are held to account for achieving ever higher standards, it is inevitable that questions are being asked about the impact of inclusion on standards.

Educational achievement and inclusion for all?

Recent government legislation and advice has done little to smooth away some of the central ambiguities and dilemmas in current education policy. Guidance from the Department for Education and Skills (DfES, 2001c), *Inclusive Schooling: Children with Special Educational Needs,* promotes the idea that all children should receive a mainstream education *unless* such education is incompatible with the 'efficient education of other children', or the wishes of the child's parents. The implication of this is that the needs of the majority should be given priority over those of the minority, however vulnerable the latter might be. Yet, in determining such incompatibility, the guidance, backed by the 2001 Special Educational Needs and Disability Act (SENDA), requires mainstream schools to take reasonable steps 'to prevent [the] child's inclusion being incompatible with the efficient education of others' (p.4). What is highly problematic, is establishing clearly the meaning of 'incompatible', 'efficient education' and 'reasonable steps'.

From the point of view of the educational achievement of children and young people identified with learning difficulties and disabilities, the Office for Standards in Education (Ofsted, 2006) has reported that it is the quality of provision, rather than whether it takes place in a mainstream or a special school, that really matters. However, the debate continues regarding the nature of the effects on the achievements of children and young people in mainstream schools who have *not* been so identified. A DfES commissioned research report on this topic encapsulates the dilemma:

> Whether inclusive schools ... do worse by many or all of their students because the presence of students with SEN distorts school processes in some way? Alternatively do such schools actually do better because they become more skilful at responding to individual differences?
>
> (Dyson *et al.*, 2004: 10)

The authors' research findings suggest that there is no straightforward relationship either way. However, once again the concepts used are not unproblematic. The terms 'inclusive schools', 'SEN', doing 'worse' and doing 'better' are, of course, open to a range of interpretations.

These tensions, and the general lack of clarity in related arguments, have been highlighted in the House of Commons Select Committee Report (July 2006) on *Special Educational Needs*. It suggests that some responsibility for this confusion lies with mixed messages from the government in terms of legislation and advice. It argues:

> What is urgently needed is for the Government to clarify its position on SEN – specifically on inclusion – and to provide national strategic direction for the future.
>
> (p.6)

And later it states:

> Regardless of the theory, in practice the evidence clearly demonstrates that SEN and the raising attainment agenda sit very uncomfortably together at present.
>
> (p.66)

Achievement and inclusion for all in the marketplace?

In England, as elsewhere, politicians have been increasingly concerned about the costs and outcomes of the education system in terms of its contribution to the nation's economic wealth and well-being. Although governments in different countries have responded in a variety of ways to these pressures, the major structural reforms that have taken place have shared certain characteristics. These have emphasised the principles of competition and choice (as noted earlier in this chapter), which together are intended to raise the academic standards of individual students, schools and nations. Mechanisms of accountability are also an essential component of this 'marketisation of education' (Power and Whitty, 1999). In England these have included the measuring of children's academic performance at ages seven, 11, 14 and 16 through standard tests and the publication of the results in performance tables.

Alongside these reforms another rather different set of large-scale educational developments has been taking place in many countries. That is, even whilst national governments have maintained this emphasis on competition, choice, accountability and standards, they have also been enacting policies to promote more inclusive educational systems. Tensions have then emerged as a result of conflicts between principles that, on the one hand, underpin market-based reforms and, on the other hand, are based on values of equity and social justice (Rouse and Florian, 1997).

England is no exception. Since the 1990s national education policy has attempted to embrace both a broad concept of inclusion *and* a specific type of marketplace reform. Ofsted now inspects and judges schools on the extent to which they are inclusive of students identified as having special educational needs, and anti-discrimination legislation (2001 SENDA; 2005 Disability Discrimination Act) has strengthened the right to a mainstream school place for children with disabilities. In addition, other initiatives, such as the government's guidance in *Inclusive Schooling: Children with Special Educational Needs* (DfES, 2001c), *Every Child Matters* (DfES, 2004a) and *Removing Barriers to Achievement* (DfES, 2004b) have together provided a legislative context for further developments in inclusive education nationally.

And yet, even in these publications there is evidence of ambiguity and tension. For example, the following statement is taken from *Barriers to Achievement*:

> Some have argued that there is a conflict between the government's school improvement and inclusion agendas. The reverse is true. Helping children with SEN to achieve is fundamental to sustaining improvements in schools' performance.
>
> (DfES, 2004b: 49)

This raises, whilst trying to dispel, the widely held concern about the incompatibility of promoting educational inclusion and raising achievement as they are presented by the government (see Chapter 2 for further discussion). It also highlights the relationship between the achievements of children 'with SEN' and a school's overall performance, thus suggesting that both inclusion and achievement are closely allied to measurable progress in key stage test results. Although this is presented in a positive manner – 'sustaining improvements' – it is not easy to see how individual schools will interpret this statement. Judgements about their overall performance may seem more pressing than concerns about a small number of children and young people, especially if they continue to have relatively low scores on national key stage tests, whatever support is given.

The House of Commons Education and Skills Committee Report (2006: 66) is highly critical of the pressure exerted by the national league tables on schools and their (un)willingness to include a broader range of students. They argue that the introduction of 'contextualised "value added" results' has not had any real impact. Referring to research from the Sutton Trust (2006) as evidence, the report notes that 'the top 200 performing non-selective state schools take far below their "fair share" of children with SEN'. It seems that other and better forms of accountability are still required.

Can achievement and inclusion – for all – work?

Nevertheless, and despite these real concerns, it does seem that some schools are able to work successfully and creatively within this ambivalent legislative system. Such schools manage to be both excellent as measured by standardised tests or external examinations, as well as committed to the continuing development of inclusive policies and practices. Our previous research (Rouse and Florian, 1996) on such schools suggests a specific refinement of the factors that are generally thought to characterise 'effective' schools – such as a common mission, a climate conducive to learning and an emphasis on learning (Stoll, 1991). In our analytic framework, effectiveness is more than efficiency or excellence for the majority. It includes the means through which the equity-excellence dilemma is mediated and, in particular, actively seeks to protect the educational needs of those children and young people who are most vulnerable and marginalised. Such a definition of effectiveness requires staff to see their schools as diverse problem-solving organisations where policies and practices are dynamic rather than static. The stories which form Chapters 5, 6, 7 and 8 illustrate some of the ways in which four different schools have set out to do so.

But, more generally, can inclusive education fulfil its promise of 'education for all', so that all children and young people have full opportunities to achieve? Can inclusive education, properly understood and implemented, reinvigorate the ideal of the comprehensive school in a twenty-first-century context? Can it help us to understand the concept of a full-service school? Does it fulfil the mandate of *Every Child Matters* which, even in its name, demands that educational inclusion and achievement are rights for all, not privileges for some? And, if so, what forms of accountability and other evidence would best support the teaching and learning of children and young people? This book sets out to explore these and other related questions.

Endnote: the structure of this book

Following this chapter the remainder of the book is in three parts. In the first (Chapters 2–4), we provide a detailed theoretical discussion about the nature of educational inclusion and achievement and how these concepts might be examined through different methodological approaches to research. We then extend this debate by describing in detail two contrasting and complementary ways of gathering evidence about achievement and inclusion. Chapter 3 focuses on the purposes, possibilities and problems of using evidence from large-scale national datasets. Chapter 4 presents the *Framework for Participation*. This provides a systematic method for collecting detailed contextual evidence to explore the relationship between inclusion and achievement at the level of individual students, classes and schools, whilst taking into account the influence of broader issues of school cultures and values and beliefs. In the second part of the book (Chapters 5–8) we present the stories of the four schools, including a brief description about how and why we undertook these particular case studies. In the final part (Chapters 9 and 10) we look across the case studies; first, to consider what we can add to the earlier theoretical discussion and second, to offer pragmatic and structured guidance to support readers who may wish to research inclusion and achievement in their own work settings.

Part I

The nature of achievement and inclusion in schools

2 Understanding the relationship between inclusion and achievement

In the previous chapter we argued that understandings of educational inclusion and achievement are partly shaped by shifting social, economic and political circumstances, whether local, national or global in nature. We suggested that in England, as elsewhere, recent government policies have put schools under increasing pressure to improve the achievement of their students, whilst also encouraging them to be more inclusive. We also noted that these policies generally present a particular and somewhat narrow interpretation of both concepts. That is, inclusion is taken to mean the process of increasing the numbers of students attending mainstream schools who, in the past, would have been prevented from doing so because of their identified special educational needs. Meanwhile, achievement is usually seen in terms only of raising academic standards as measured by national Key Stage tests and other examinations, rather than the broader areas of achievement as outlined in Box 1.1.

Improving both inclusion and achievement are, of course, worthwhile and important educational aims and this dual focus on the most vulnerable students and on all students is a welcome development. However, the lack of depth of clarity about meanings can make it difficult for teachers to know how best to proceed in developing policies and practices that will encourage schools to be both highly inclusive in their student intake whilst supporting the highest achievements from all their students. As the Audit Commission (2002: 2) reports, 'Schools have struggled to balance pressures to raise standards of attainment and to become more inclusive'. Indeed, there continues to be widespread concern that the inclusion in mainstream schools of students identified as having special educational needs negatively affects the achievement of other students in that school and lowers academic standards overall.

In this chapter we continue to explore the tensions in this relationship and discuss how they might be resolved. The chapter is divided into three main sections. We begin by examining the concept of inclusion; how it is understood by practitioners working in schools and as it is presented in government documents and in recent research. In so doing we consider a number of associated ideas such as exclusion, integration, special educational needs, difficulties in learning and disability as well as broader notions of social and economic inclusion and exclusion.

Similarly, in the second section we examine the concept of achievement and its meanings, as well as the related notions of academic standards, progress and performance, plus broader understandings of educational achievement. Currently, in England, the government's core policy for services for children and young people is *Every Child Matters: Change for Children* (DfES, 2004a: 4). In this, 'enjoying and achieving' is identified as one of five major outcomes that are key to 'well-being in children and in later life'. This then requires some consideration of the purposes of schools more generally and our aspirations for what children should achieve (and enjoy achieving) during 11 or so years of compulsory education and beyond. Skills in literacy and numeracy are undoubtedly important, but so too are other achievements which may be more intangible but not necessarily less valuable; these might include, for example, developing self-esteem, self-efficacy, resilience, social skills, creativity, tolerance and empathy.

In the final section of the chapter we bring together these two concepts and consider the relationship between them. We reflect on how different conceptual understandings produce different methodological approaches to the measurement, assessment and monitoring of both inclusion and achievement in schools and how these, in turn, enable different stories to be told about their relationship to each other. We consider the nature of schools that are able to both be highly inclusive in terms of their intake of students and encourage the highest achievements from all their students.

Examining the concept of educational inclusion and inclusive education

Educational inclusion and inclusive education are complex concepts that are difficult to define and are open to a range of understandings. These variations have developed out of different historical, geographical and theoretical contexts, although they clearly share certain principles based on notions of equity and social justice. Furthermore, inclusion is closely linked to other terms – such as integration, special educational needs and exclusion – which are also susceptible to differences of interpretations. Such differences inevitably affect the ways in which levels of inclusion in schools are assessed, as well as how the impact of inclusion on students' learning is evaluated.

Inclusion and integration

In some contexts, the term inclusion has become associated with issues of integration although, as noted above, this term is also open to a variety of interpretations. At its most straightforward integration requires that a student from a special school be given access to – be included in – a mainstream school for part or all of his or her education. In practice, however, integration can take many forms. It may be locational and/or social only, or it may also include partial or full access to a school's academic curriculum. It may involve a student attending a neighbourhood school or it may be another mainstream school outside his/her local community. In these ways the term inclusion is used simply to describe the act of physically locating students designated as having special educational needs in mainstream schools. For example, in the document *Excellence for All Children* (DfEE, 1997: 5), the government outlined six themes, of which one is, 'The inclusion of children with SEN within mainstream schooling'. Here the concept of inclusion is concerned with a minority of students who are perceived as having particular learning difficulties which, in the past, may have resulted in them attending special schools. It can be seen that sometimes the concepts of integration and inclusion have become blurred.

This trend to place children in mainstream schools has developed out of an increasing dissatisfaction amongst some educationalists about the appropriateness of providing segregated education in special schools. Arguments for integration have been concerned with both philosophical notions of equality of rights and practical considerations about the efficiency of running two parallel school systems (Swann, 1988; Dessent, 1987; Sebba and Ainscow, 1996; Thomas *et al.*, 1998). Some argue that mainstream classroom teachers should take responsibility for providing the necessary support to help all students overcome barriers to learning with specialist input as needed; others believe that specialists should work directly with learners; still others argue that specialist facilities and schools are the best way to provide for some children and young people. To date there has been no satisfactory resolution to this debate although numerous approaches to inclusive education for students identified as having special educational needs have emerged.

Inclusion and special educational needs

In England, following the Warnock Report (DES, 1978), the 1981 Education Act attempted to leave behind the notion of applying categories of handicap to some children and young people and introduced instead the concept of special educational need. This task involved loosening definitions and accepting the interactive nature of disability and learning difficulty. The term, special educational needs, is an elusive one meaning different things to different people in different places and concerning many kinds of difficulties in learning, from those relating to particular physical impairments to learning and behavioural difficulties experienced by some learners compared with other similar learners.

Over time special educational need has become a kind of super category covering about 20 per cent of children. Definitions have become circular. A child has a special educational need if they receive special needs provision and in turn special needs provision is defined as 'additional to' or 'different from' what is normally available. Thus, professional (and often parental) efforts are often focused on trying to secure more resources rather than on pedagogical and curriculum concerns.

Schools and local authorities have responded differently to this pressure, because of different local histories and funding mechanisms. Consequently, patterns of provision for meeting special educational needs are hugely variable across England. Indeed, there are sizeable differences between local authorities and schools in terms of who is identified as having special educational needs, and where and how these needs are met. These variations have been consistently reported since the implementation of the 1981 Education Act (see, for example, Audit Commission, 1992; Lunt and Evans, 1994; Norwich, 1997). In England and Wales the variation of the numbers of children who receive statements is five-fold across different local authorities (Audit Commission, 2002) and the variation of the percentage of children with statements of special educational needs attending special schools is 24-fold (Rustemier and Vaughn, 2005).

Thus, for many, inclusion has been concerned with the placement in mainstream schools of students who have been identified as having special educational needs, and who might, in the past, have attended a special school or other provision separate or different from the majority of students. As this view has gained currency in policy, the term inclusion or 'inclusive education' has begun to be used as a replacement for 'special needs education'. This is particularly important because, as Tomlinson (1982) convincingly showed, 'special needs' are artefacts of mainstream education.

As a result of growing demands on mainstream schools to raise standards, increasing numbers of children and young people are being identified as having learning difficulties, because their low academic achievements are cause for concern. Indeed, as Davis and Florian (2004) have argued, it is only when the difficulties which students experience exceed the capacity of schools to respond, that students are considered to have special educational needs and are deemed to require specialist support. In this way, low academic achievement can become pathologised and schools are then able to maintain their focus on those students who are potentially high achievers (Gillborn and Youdell, 2000). This is one reason why many proponents of inclusion reject special education provision as a form of discrimination.

Inclusion and exclusion

As with the concepts of integration and special educational needs, the educational meanings associated with the concept of exclusion have a particular historical and cultural context. In England, the government introduced the term to describe the removal of a student from school either temporarily or permanently for disciplinary reasons (1986 Education Act, Number Two). This replaced the use of the terms suspension and expulsion. Until recently, many educationalists have also confined their usage of the word to this specific technical sense (Stirling, 1992; Parsons, 1996; Blyth and Milner, 1997; Hayden, 1997). The emphasis, then, is on children's physical absence from school. This parallels the notion of integration/inclusion as being concerned with a student being placed in a mainstream or in a special school. This understanding of exclusion received particular attention throughout the 1990s, as official figures for the number of students excluded from schools for disciplinary reasons increased significantly (Parsons, 1996). There has also been concern about the over-representation of certain groups of students in these figures (DfEE, 1999).

For example, Blyth and Milner (1997) highlight the disproportionate number of Afro-Caribbean young people excluded from school and in particular teenage boys. Stirling (1992), meanwhile, has focused on the high number of 'looked after' children and young people who are removed from schools.

Nevertheless, there has also been a shift towards a broader conceptualisation of educational exclusion. Sebba and Ainscow (1996: 8), for example, describe 'The more subtle or hidden processes of discrimination related to factors such as socio-economic circumstances, gender or race'. Booth (1997) highlights some of the ways in which a student may be unofficially kept out of school. He describes such processes as 'exclusion by default – active and passive' (p.32); that is, those students who are excluded because schools have not actively sought to include them. He provides a number of examples such as traveller children, truants, pregnant schoolgirls and school-aged mothers. He goes on to argue that exclusion relates to how children and young people are valued and devalued within their schools (p.35). Similarly, outside education, the concept of exclusion has also been given a broader application: that of being excluded from society. For example, the government set up the Social Exclusion Unit in 1997 for the purpose of scrutinising poverty, housing and unemployment, as well as education.

If, as Slee (2005) has argued, inclusion can be seen as a challenge to exclusion for whatever reason (race, gender, sexual orientation, religion) then it is important to note that these challenges have tended to follow a pattern of exposure to discrimination. This has led to anti-discrimination laws and positive discrimination policies which have paved the way for more integrated educational provision. Thus, a notion of equality underpins the concept of inclusion that sees education as a human right and disability as a social construction.

Inclusion and government perspectives in England

Writing in 2002, Booth and Smith describe the number of government documents, in England, which discuss the notion of inclusion as being 'unprecedented'. They also note that, within these texts, a range of perspectives, understandings and meanings are associated with this term. Box 2.1 offers a summary of just some of the areas they have identified. This range of meanings reflects much of our discussion in this section so far. However, such variety makes recognising the influence of government policies on inclusion in schools, let alone evaluating and developing them, problematic: not only for the government but also for teachers in schools who are expected to put them into practice.

There are, however, two main ideas embedded in the list in Box 2.1, although these too may bring further tensions. On the one hand, there is a sharp focus on individual and groups of children who have been identified as being particularly vulnerable to processes of exclusion: those designated as having special educational needs, or likely to experience discrimination, or living in poverty, and so forth. On the other hand, inclusion is presented as being central to the educational experiences of all students. Beginning with the Green Paper, *Excellence for All Children* (DfEE, 1997), and continuing in all of its policy

Box 2.1   Summary of governmental usage of inclusion

- special needs education
- access to and participation within mainstream schools for students categorised as having special educational needs and/or disabilities
- social inclusion/exclusion relating to issues such as truancy, behaviour or looked after children
- issues of racial and other forms of discrimination
- community stresses brought about by poverty, lack of housing, etc.
- inclusion as an underlying general principle for education
- reducing exclusionary pressures on, and supporting the participation of, all children and young people in schools.

(based on Booth and Smith, 2002)

documents, the government has suggested that there is no single best route to inclusion. It has consistently proposed retaining traditional approaches focusing on a small number of children and young people (such as the identification and assessment of special educational needs, individual education plans, statements and specialist facilities for those who choose them), whilst also advocating for more comprehensive approaches that are inclusive of all learners.

The distinction between some and all children and young people is important because it parallels government policy and advice on promoting educational achievement. That is, there is a focus in government educational documents both on individuals/groups who are vulnerable to underachievement in terms of scores on national tests, and on 'raising standards' in those tests across whole school cohorts, local authorities and nationally. And, in terms of measuring and monitoring both inclusion and achievement, those test results are presented as key evidence. There is a circularity in this process which may lead to confusion between 'means' and 'ends'. This is discussed further in Chapter 3.

Inclusion as a process: improving schools for all

More than a decade ago, Ainscow (1991), amongst others, put forward the view that the development of more inclusive schools corresponded with strategies intended to bring about school improvement more generally. However, the school improvement movement has become entangled in notions of school effectiveness and this in turn has been associated with the drive to raise academic standards at the expense of other outcomes, and differences between learners are not necessarily considered important. In England, the problem facing those committed to developing inclusive schools has been about mediating the tension between the demands for excellence in academic achievements with the principle of equity. To be equitable does not require a denial of difference. There is no doubt that there are differences between learners. The key questions are, as Minow (1990) has asked: what counts as difference and what difference does difference make?

The Index for Inclusion (Booth *et al.*, 2000), for example, calls for a broader restructuring of mainstream schools to ensure they are more responsive to student diversity. Such an approach focuses on expanding a school's capacity to improve its response to all its students, based on a social interactive model for teaching and learning. The writers emphasise that inclusion is 'a set of never-ending processes' (p.12) by which a school strives to increase the participation of its members, rather than a fixed state that can never be attained. Or, as Emanuelsson (1998: 72) argues, inclusion is about working towards an unachievable goal in which 'there will always be new territories to conquer'.

More recently, Ainscow *et al.* (2004) have argued that focusing on students identified as having special educational needs leads to a narrow conceptualisation of inclusion because processes of inclusion and exclusion take many forms and affect many different kinds of children. They argue that educational research should be concerned with understanding the practices that arise when teachers set out to identify and remove the barriers to participation and learning experienced by students. We strongly concur with this school improvement view of inclusion and agree that the focus is rightly placed on removing barriers to participation and learning. However, we also acknowledge that, in practice, such barriers are often construed as 'special needs', not least because, as already noted, this remains a key term used by national and local governments to determine additional resources and other provision. It is therefore important to recognise that for teachers 'inclusion' and 'special needs' are not separate representations or constructions of learning difficulty. Moreover, whilst the concept of 'special needs' may pathologise some learners, rejecting it does not necessarily help practitioners to address the structural problems that create those 'needs' in the first place. A more nuanced and relational way of considering how schools can respond to difference is needed and we discuss this in more depth later in this chapter.

Examining the concept of achievement in education

It is axiomatic to state that a fundamental aim of any school is to ensure that all its students achieve at the highest possible levels. However, beyond this commonplace understanding, questions about what is actually meant by achievement and which achievements are of greatest value, for individual students and across whole schools and even nations, remain problematic. Furthermore, assessments of achievement depend on a set of outcome measures against which schools may then be held accountable. Therefore, decisions need to be made about which outcomes are important and how they will be judged. Distinguishing between standards, attainments and progress is also necessary.

Achievement, academic standards and progress

Standards in education are often considered to be a set of minimum performance criteria, usually in basic areas of the curriculum (such as literacy and numeracy), that specify what all children should know, understand and be able to do by certain ages. The current trend to specify levels of attainment is part of an international movement of 'standards based reform', which is intended not only to raise academic standards but also to increase the accountability of teachers and schools. In this sense, standards are not concerned with starting points but rather with outcomes. Achievement on the other hand might be defined as being about the progress made by learners over time. Thus it is possible for students to have achieved well, given their starting point, but not to have reached the (arbitrary) standards as pre-specified by performance criteria. When this distinction between the two terms is considered at the school level it is possible to understand the seemingly paradoxical claim that in some schools, whilst standards are low, achievement is high.

Most students will increase their level of achievement as they pass through school, although the amount of progress over time will differ between individuals. Whilst progress is not necessarily linear, virtually all children will learn new skills in literacy and numeracy, they will acquire new knowledge across a range of curriculum areas and they will also develop socially and emotionally as they move through school. This increase in achievement and development can be thought of as progress.

However, progress is affected by many factors in addition to what happens in school. Improvements in achievement are associated with increased maturity and are influenced by the environments in which students learn, live and grow. School is but one of these environments, which includes the nature of the curriculum, the quality of teaching, the kinds of expectations that adults have of students and students have of themselves and of each other, the systems of assessment (including how children are assessed as having special educational needs), relationships with adults and other children, the organisation of student groupings, the organisation and availability of learning support, and so on. These and many other factors affect the progress of individuals and groups of students.

Achievement, progress and value-added

Judgements about achievement based on numerical comparative data, and when defined as progress, require value-added rather than raw scores. In this sense progress provides a fairer as well as a more meaningful indication of a school's success in supporting the learning of its students than measures of absolute standards only. This is particularly true of schools that include a high proportion of students who have been identified as having special educational needs and that are likely, therefore, to be working with children and young people whose starting points are generally lower than those of others.

Whilst all schools intend their students to achieve, it is difficult to identify the exact ways in which different schools successfully set out to support students' progress. However, if one school increases the achievement level of its students more than another school, then its students can be seen as gaining an additional advantage. It is this relative advantage that has come to be called 'value-added'. Calculating value-added involves a procedure that accounts for a range of variables thought to be associated with attainment. The measure that remains, after the other variables that might influence students' achievements have been accounted for, is the value-added score. It will be influenced by many factors such as students' efforts, motivation, health, home experiences and help from others, in addition to the teaching provided by the school. Nevertheless, it is claimed that such an approach is the best available indicator of the net effect that schools have (Benton, 2003).

Achievement, comparative data, standards and 'league tables'

The gathering of comparative data on students' achievements is a central feature of many educational systems throughout the world, although it may be collected at different levels (or units of analysis) and used for a range of different purposes. For example, comparisons might be at the level of:

- the individual child, for the purpose of improving teaching and learning
- the group, to help inform judgements about resource allocation
- the class, phase or Key Stage, department, or the school, for accountability purposes
- the local authority, as outlined in the National Performance Framework for SEN: designed to give authorities easy access to a variety of datasets and indicators to support monitoring, self-review and development.

As part of the international 'standards based reform', noted earlier, comparative information on the academic achievement of students and schools is collected and then is often made publicly available. Doing so is intended to underpin the notions of accountability, competition and choice in education.

In England, for example, performance tables give average levels for individual schools and across LAs as measured by Key Stages 2 and 3 tests and GCSEs at Key Stage 4. From 2002, there have been some improvements to the way the figures are compiled by the DfES to form the (now called) Achievement and Attainment Tables. That is, Key Stage to Key Stage value-added measures are used to indicate progress from one stage to the next, rather than simply using absolute outcome measures at the end of one particular Key Stage. The DfES (2006) claims that such value-added approaches are fairer than using raw outcomes, since the average level of attainment of students on entry to different schools can vary considerably.

Individual schools are also increasingly expected to make use of information from available national datasets to raise overall standards as well as identify groups of students who might be 'underperforming'. For example, in England, the government has strongly advised schools to draw on data from PANDA (Performance and Assessment Data) and, more recently, from the PLASC (Pupil Level Annual School Census). Such datasets can be helpful in so far as they allow comparisons to be made that take some account of the differing circumstances of individual schools. PANDA does so, for example, by comparing schools that have similar proportions of children who are eligible for free school meals and also by measuring progress in test results (or value-added) rather than absolute scores.

Furthermore, access to the data gathered through the PLASC now lets schools make more finely graded distinctions based on other factors that might affect the progress students make in a school; what the DfES describes as 'contextual value-added'. The current models are intended to allow individual and groups of children to be compared across a range of contextual factors, such as mobility, date of birth, gender, categories of identified special educational needs, first language, ethnicity, measures of social/economic deprivation and so forth. The PLASC also allows schools to track attainment, across time, in terms of prior attainments of individual students as well as the average and range of prior attainment across a school (Key Stages 2–3, 2–4 and 3–4 only).

However, a number of assumptions about progress underpin this approach and the production of numerical comparative data has only limited value for teachers. The presentation of such information is in the form of: last year, this year, next year; our school, other (similar) schools, all schools; this child, these children, other children. As such it can only offer some insights into questions that ask 'what', rather than 'why' this is so and 'how' a school might develop (raise standards) in the future. A more detailed discussion of the uses and misuses of national datasets to evaluate and develop more inclusive and higher achieving schools is provided in Chapter 3.

Achievement for all: monitoring individuals and groups

Historically, one of the main areas of focus for special education provision has been the development of assessment systems intended to demonstrate and record progress made by individuals. This can be seen, for example, in approaches such as daily monitoring and precision teaching, which use graphical indicators of progress. Whilst such methods can be powerful indicators of improvement by individuals, they have been less useful at the group level because of the difficulty of aggregating personally referenced assessment information. In addition, these approaches raise difficulties if they are also to be used for broader accountability purposes. Meanwhile, systems used to monitor groups generally involve ranking or standardised measures that are often too insensitive to demonstrate progress in the achievements of students who find learning most difficult.

In England, there has been growing concern about the inappropriateness of the Key Stage national curriculum tests for some children and young people and, in particular, for those who are unlikely to achieve above level two at the end of Key Stage 4 (QCA/DfES, 2001). In response to this the P-scales have been developed and introduced into schools (DfES, 2006). The intention of this system has been to provide more finely differentiated outcomes for such students whilst at the same time allowing them to be assessed within the unified system of accountability that includes all learners. The purposes of P-scales are discussed in greater detail in Chapter 3.

There are other broader criticisms of the negative effect of Key Stage tests on the achievements of individual and groups of children and young people. Of particular concern is that the publication of league tables and expectations about raising standards puts schools under pressure to target certain students who may be borderline between one level and the next. Schools may then provide extra teaching to 'push' these students into the next level, at the expense of other students whose progress is less valued because less visible in league tables (Gillborn and Youdell, 2000). A related concern is the effect on the self-esteem of students whose anxiety about their performance in national tests may contribute to their understanding of themselves as poor learners (Reay and Wiliam, 1999). Many teachers are also anxious about how they will be judged as professionals when the results for their classes are made public. James (2006) argues that some teachers are being placed under unacceptable levels of stress because of the pressure on them to attain ever higher results.

These effects of national tests cannot easily be measured; however, it seems unlikely that they will help to raise standards in the longer term, even if test results improve in the short term. As Apple (2006: 76) notes:

> Of course, there are poor schools and there are ineffective practices in schools. However, the reduction of education to scores on what are often inadequate measures, often used in technically and educationally inappropriate ways for comparative purposes, has some serious consequences.

There is a danger, then, that national testing systems, intended to raise the academic standards of all students, may actually impede the progress of some students and thus perpetuate inequalities between those who are perceived as high achievers academically and those who are not. Furthermore, because one type of achievement appears straightforward to 'measure' does not make that particular achievement more valuable than others that are less easily evaluated. Nor does 'measuring' achievement, in itself, bring about improvement. There is truth in the saying, 'You don't fatten a pig by weighing it'.

Achievement and broader conceptualisations

Educational achievement is not limited to academic attainment and therefore it seems essential to consider ways of understanding other achievements, such as students' social, emotional and creative development, and how progress in these might best be evaluated and against which outcomes. In England, guidance from the government (DfEE, 2000: 3) notes that a key aim of a school's curriculum must be to promote students' self-esteem and emotional well-being and to help them to form and maintain worthwhile and satisfying relationships, based on respect for themselves and for others. Similar achievements can be identified in government policy on the role of 'citizenship' in education, although with an emphasis on achievement outcomes relating to the well-being of communities and society rather than that of individuals.

More recently, the government has established *Every Child Matters* as its overarching policy for education, health and social services for children and young people (DfES, 2004a). This is underpinned by five major outcomes that are key to 'well-being in children and in later life' and are presented as the joint responsibility of all professionals who work with children. These are:

1   Being healthy
2   Staying safe
3   Enjoying and achieving
4   Making a positive contribution
5   Achieving economic well-being

In the Ofsted (2005b) Framework for the Inspection of Children's Services, a set of subsidiary outcome measures are provided for each one, plus a number of key judgements. The latter includes a particular focus on more vulnerable children and young people who may require additional support to attain the specified outcomes; for example, children who are in the care of social services ('looked after') and/or are designated as having learning difficulties and/or disabilities. Box 2.2 provides an example of the above for the first of the five major outcomes: 'being healthy'.

Notwithstanding the importance of all the elements included, this helps to illustrate some of the difficulties encountered by professionals when measuring outcomes which are neither assessed according to numerical scores, nor linear in progression. For example, a child's physical health can deteriorate in ways such that literacy skills, once acquired, are unlikely to be lost. And, if it is difficult to make judgements about physical health over time, then how much more so is measuring the achievement and maintenance of students' mental and emotional health?

Box 2. 2   Being healthy

Outcomes:
  Children and young people:
  • are physically healthy;
  • are mentally and emotionally healthy;
  • are sexually healthy;
  • have healthy lifestyles;
  • choose not to take illegal drugs.

Key judgements:
  • parents and carers receive support to keep their children healthy
  • healthy lifestyles are promoted for children and young people
  • action is taken to promote children and young people's physical health
  • action is taken to promote children and young people's mental health
  • looked after children's health needs are addressed
  • the health needs of children and young people with learning difficulties and/or disabilities are addressed.

(Ofsted, 2005b)

Achievement, broader conceptualisations and accountability

How far are schools able to contribute to the fulfilment of these outcomes? And how will they judge the success, or otherwise, of their actions? It is quite clear that the government expects all teachers and schools to be accountable in terms of promoting all five key outcomes, and not, as might be expected, to be concerned predominantly with the third one: 'enjoying and achieving' (DfES, 2004a). This is unambiguously reflected in the recently changed arrangements for the inspection of schools in England, which now judge schools in terms of the contribution they make to support their students' 'well-being' (Ofsted, 2005c). One section of the SEF (self-evaluation form), which each school is expected to complete prior to an Ofsted inspection, is concerned with the following question: 'How good is the overall personal development and well-being of the learners?' Box 2.3 shows the five subsidiary questions which schools must address in response to this. Each is clearly based on one of the five key outcomes from *Every Child Matters*.

The government does not present these broader achievements as being additional to the raising of academic standards, but as integral to them.

Box 2.3   Extract from Ofsted SEF (section 4)

How good is the overall personal development and well-being of the learners?

1   To what extent do learners adopt healthy lifestyles?
- whether learners take adequate physical exercise, and eat and drink healthily
- learners' growing understanding of how to live a healthy lifestyle
2   To what extent do learners feel safe and adopt safe practices?
- whether learners feel safe from bullying and racist incidents
- the extent to which learners have confidence to talk to staff and others when they feel at risk
3   How much do learners enjoy their education?
- take account of learners' attitudes, behaviour and attendance
- learners' spiritual, moral, social, emotional and cultural development
4   How well do learners make a positive contribution to the community?
- learners' growing understanding of their rights and responsibilities, and of those of others
- how well learners express their views and contribute to communal activities
5   How well do learners prepare for their future economic well-being?
- how well learners develop skills and personal qualities that will enable them to achieve future economic well-being

---

Pupil performance and well-being go hand in hand. Pupils can't learn if they don't feel safe or if health problems are allowed to create barriers. And doing well in education is the most effective route for young people out of poverty and disaffection.

(DfES, 2004a: 1)

Examining inclusion in the context of achievement

In this section we look more closely at the relationship between students' academic achievements and their inclusion in schools. However, as is already evident in the chapter so far, it is not easy to discuss one concept without making reference to the other. For example, in the quotation at the end of the previous section, the government makes explicit the relationship between 'pupil performance and well-being'. In doing so their presentation of well-being appears to share certain characteristics with those we would use to describe processes of inclusion in schools. And their notions of 'barriers' to 'well-being' are, we would argue, similar in some ways to our understanding of processes of exclusion. Furthermore, whilst the *Every Child Matters* policy concerns all students (that is, 'every child'), it also focuses on those who may be particularly at risk in terms of encountering those barriers. Similarly, in this book, we are interested in how schools can raise the achievements of all children and young people whilst safeguarding the inclusion of those who are more vulnerable to the pressures of exclusion.

The relationship between inclusion and achievement: current concerns

It is clear that inclusion and achievement are contested and problematic concepts and that the relationship between them has been subjected to great scrutiny in recent years (Ofsted, 2004; Dyson *et al.*, 2004; Rouse and Florian, 2006). There are a number of reasons for this interest. Despite this lack of clarity about meanings, the idea of both increasing inclusion and raising standards remains at the heart of current government policies for reforming schools in England. Meanwhile, there are those who have suggested that inclusion and high standards may be incompatible (Lunt and Norwich, 1999; Audit Commission, 2002). If achievement is understood in terms of standards, and these are defined as academic outcomes, which are judged against absolute or comparative criteria and across a narrow range of curriculum subjects, then this argument may be true. But if achievement is defined differently, other conclusions may then be possible, and different questions will then need to be asked.

Understanding the relationship between educational inclusion and achievement is of importance to educationalists for other reasons. Many of these are at the heart of concerns about where and how children and young people should be educated. These include: the pressures on schools brought about by increased accountability; the justification for allocating additional resources to groups of students; the introduction of national strategies to improve teaching and learning more generally; the development of evidence based practice; unease about the morale of teachers and the motivation of students. Furthermore, these concerns also come at a time when advances in technology have increased researchers' ability to handle large amounts of data, thus making it possible to frame questions that could not have been answered in the past.

Previous attempts to explore these issues have been restricted by the nature of the data available and the problematic nature of carrying out such research. For example, Lunt and Norwich (1999) used data from the 1998 GCSE league tables to examine the relationship between the proportion of students identified as having special educational needs in a school and its position in the table. They found that schools with higher percentages of such identified students had lower GCSE performance levels. Although their findings appear to support arguments regarding the incompatibility of inclusion and achievement, other considerations need to be taken into account. Their study did not consider the starting points of students (the data were not available at the time of their study) so that absolute scores rather than students' progress were used. Nor were they able to use alternative performance indicators which might have produced different results. Moreover, the majority of the schools with lower performance levels were mixed comprehensives, without selective admission policies, and they also tended to be concentrated within a subset of county LAs suggesting that LA policy and practice, and perhaps demography, are important factors in what schools are able to achieve.

More recently, technological advances have enabled researchers to use national data in far more complex ways so as to examine the relationship between inclusion and achievement (Dyson *et al.*, 2004; Rouse and Florian, 2006). As we have noted already in this chapter, it is now possible in England to examine the performance of individuals over their whole school careers. In addition, 'value-added' information about student progress from one Key Stage of education to the next Key Stage using assessment data from the national pupil database (NPD), can be combined with demographic data (such as socio-economic status, ethnicity, first language spoken and identified special educational needs) from the PLASC. Merging this data makes it possible to explore issues of inclusion and achievement in ways which have not been possible previously. This is discussed in more detail in Chapter 3.

The relationship between inclusion and achievement: conceptualising inclusive schools as high achieving schools

A fundamental question arising from the apparent tension between equity and excellence is: how can a school become equitable for diverse groups of learners (that is, inclusive because they accommodate difference) as well as be excellent for all (that is, demonstrate achievement gains for all children and young people)? Our earlier research on inclusive practice in secondary schools (Florian and Rouse, 2001) has led to a conceptualisation of inclusive schools as those that meet the dual criteria of enrolling a diverse student population *and* of constantly seeking to improve the achievements of all their students. This definition therefore supports both the entitlement of all children and young people to a mainstream placement, whilst also taking into account the nature of school and classroom policies and practices, which set out to be increasingly responsive to the learning and participation of all students.

Therefore, our approach to understanding this process of becoming more inclusive is to study the work of practitioners who are committed to the principle of inclusion and who see their schools as problem-solving organisations where policy and practice are dynamic rather than static. As we conceive it, their work involves continually reinventing inclusion to make it happen in their school and classrooms and for their students and colleagues. Our research suggests that such schools can be 'effective schools' as defined by the competitive marketplace philosophies that underpin mainstream education in many countries. We have used this understanding of developing inclusive schools to help us to identify the four schools which comprise the case studies presented in Chapters 5, 6, 7 and 8. Each has found a range of ways to mediate the tensions produced by the clash of conflicting philosophies that underpin inclusion and marketplace reform. The challenge is not to see these schools as exceptions in the face of the widespread popular belief that the inclusion of students designated as having special educational needs in mainstream schools has a negative effect on the academic achievements of other students in that school. Our interest in them is not that they are exceptional in this regard, but that they provide rich evidence to enable concepts of achievement and inclusion to be examined.

We have explored these schools as complete systems, rather than applied a checklist of pre-specified criteria about what might count as inclusion. This approach reflects two other important aspects of our conceptual understanding. First, different schools, quite properly, use different approaches to become increasingly inclusive because they must respond to the particular circumstances of their school and the needs of their students. Second, any exploration of issues of inclusion (or achievement) demands the careful consideration of the underlying effects of a school's culture (Black-Hawkins, 2002). Furthermore, these two points are closely linked. School-based decisions about policies and practices intended to develop more inclusionary processes are determined within the culture of that school. Meanwhile, existing policies and practices help to shape the school's culture and the values and beliefs held by its members.

Stoll (1999: 47) has argued that:

> Real improvement cannot come from anywhere other than from within schools themselves, and 'within' is a complex web of values and beliefs, norms, social and power relationships and emotions.

Above all, relationships – amongst students, amongst staff and between staff and students – are at the heart of understanding and developing inclusion in a school. This is not to promote a naïve, sentimental approach to education, in which expectations about achievement are suppressed, but to acknowledge that teaching and learning take place within the context of human relationships, shaped by individuals' and institutional values and beliefs. Therefore, the emotional lives of members of a school's community cannot be ignored. Indeed, the activities of a school itself create and shape deeply felt emotions and these responses help to form and are formed by its values and beliefs. As O'Hanlon (2000: 23) notes:

> The emotions should not play an inferior role in our deliberations about education. ... Emotion and its associated moods permeate our experience and are not ... interruptions or brief moments of madness that punctuate an otherwise cool and calm journey of rational objectivity.

If feelings such as fear, humiliation, failure, intolerance and anger are ignored then barriers to inclusion and achievement are strengthened. Similarly, these processes cannot be developed if pleasure, success, happiness and confidence are not valued and if respect, responsibility, kindness and resilience are not encouraged. The ordinariness of everyday school life invokes all these emotions in students and staff.

Therefore, we are guided by Gould's (1996) insight that trends (in this case towards greater inclusion) are about changes in variation within complete systems, rather than a single entity or process moving directionally. Our focus is not on the existing inequities in current national systems but on the ways in which individual schools set out to accommodate variations amongst all their learners so that all can achieve, whether or not they have been identified as having disabilities, learning difficulties or special educational needs. These concerns are discussed in detail in Chapter 4 and are integral to the case studies.

3   National datasets

What do they tell us about achievement and inclusion?

Until recently, questions about whether the inclusion of students identified as having special educational needs in mainstream schools has an impact on achievement (by others as well as those so identified) have been difficult to answer, as the necessary data have not been available. In England, the Department for Education and Skills (DfES) now produces a national pupil database (NPD) every year that contains information about the attainments of individuals together with demographic information compiled from information submitted in the Pupil Level Annual Schools Census (PLASC). These innovations have made it possible to produce a single dataset containing specific information about the attainment, socio-economic status (through eligibility for free school meals and post code), ethnicity, gender, age, first language spoken and special educational needs of all students. Every child in the country has been allocated a unique pupil number (UPN), which means that individuals can be tracked over their whole school careers. In theory, the availability of these data now allows questions to be answered about whether placement and provision influence performance for individuals and for different groups of children.

The development of national datasets is, in part, a response to increasing international demands for higher standards and accountability for all children (Malmgren *et al.*, 2005). Also, in many countries, there is increasing pressure for policies and practices to be evidence-based (Odom *et al.*, 2005; Evidence for Policy and Practice Information and Co-ordinating Centre (EPPI), http://eppi.ioe.ac.uk/cms/), together with an emphasis on finding out about 'what works'. These pressures have also increased the need for meaningful data about which children are receiving additional services and provision, such as special education, and for monitoring the learning and attainment of those children who receive such support (DfES, 2003b; Ofsted, 2004; OECD, 2005). There is greater interest than ever to know whether the extra investment of time and money in special education services leads to improved outcomes for learners. It is also argued that these data will allow patterns of attainment for individuals, as well as for particular groups, to be revealed. In the past such patterns would have been 'buried' in the aggregated school level data. In addition the DfES (2005b) has produced *Leading on Inclusion*, a professional development resource pack for local authorities, designed to encourage schools to take a more strategic approach to managing inclusion based on a process of data-driven school self-evaluation.

At first sight the availability of these new national datasets appears to be a positive development for researchers, policy makers and others interested in these matters. This chapter explores the opportunities presented by them and some of the conceptual and technical problems involved in their use to explore questions about achievement and inclusion. Obviously some of these concerns arise from the difficulty in defining the terms inclusion and achievement, but in addition there are fundamental problems and limitations with these data that need to be understood if they are to make a useful contribution to an understanding of achievement and inclusion.

The national pupil database

The national pupil database (NPD) in England contains data on virtually every child in the country. As previously mentioned, it includes personal information on date of birth, gender, ethnicity, first language spoken, home post code, eligibility for free school meals and special needs status. There are now two elements to the special needs information. The first relates to the 'level' of special needs support required by the child. This ranges from no special needs, through 'school action', to 'school action plus' where help is needed from outside the school, and finally to a 'Statement of special education needs', a legal document that is intended to specify the type of provision that should be made available to the child. Second, schools are asked to specify a child's primary area of need. The identification and categorisation of students by type of special need presents particular difficulties given the interactive nature of the concept of special needs, and the consequential lack of specificity of the definitions. In addition, there are difficulties with the assessment of educational progress and also with whether the focus for accountability purposes should be on individuals, groups or institutions. The datasets also contain technical problems arising from the structure of the datasets themselves, how variables are defined and treated, and what analyses are possible given concerns about the validity and reliability of the data. Nevertheless, these datasets are being used at a number of different levels to improve accountability and to help inform the decision making process.

Not only are the data being used by schools, but also at local authority level. The first National Performance Framework (NPF) for special educational needs was introduced in 2002. Its aim was to provide key data for local authorities (LAs) across a range of indicators relating to children identified as having special educational needs, thus enabling individual LAs to compare their performance with similar LAs for the purpose of self-review and evaluation. This work is part of a wider programme to improve accountability for children and young people designated as having special educational needs, including the requirements on LAs to provide information on their special needs provision and funding arrangements, including delegated budgets. Unfortunately the NPF is only available to LAs, and not to schools. However, a number of LAs have been collaborating on the development and use of such data to benchmark their performance through approaches developed by the Special Educational Needs Regional Partnerships and much of this work is available online (see, for example, the work of the London Regional Partnership Framework for Inclusive Education: Data Profiling Project, 2004, http://www.londonrp.org.ok/rpts_pubs/reportsandpubs_index.asp). Although fascinating, such uses of the NPD are not without their problems.

Problems with definitions and differential rates of identification between schools and local authorities

As noted in Chapter 2, the term special educational needs covers an array of difficulties. This is highlighted in the *Special Educational Needs Code of Practice* which

> does not assume that there are hard and fast categories of special educational need ... [and] recognises that there is a wide spectrum of special educational needs that are frequently inter-related, although there are also specific needs that usually relate directly to particular types of impairment.
>
> (DfES, 2001b: 85, §7.52)

As a result, numerous approaches to provision have been developed and the extent to which these require a designation of special educational needs is variable. Moreover, variations in context produce different ideas about who has special needs. Furthermore, it would be unwise to compare the progress of two students with a statement of special needs where, for example, one has a statement because of profound and multiple learning difficulties and the other has a statement for a specific learning difficulty (Florian *et al.*, 2004).

Because definitions of special needs can only be understood in the context in which they occur and because various schools and LAs have their own particular ways of defining special needs and organising responses, it is not surprising that rates of identification and patterns of provision are hugely variable across England. Different local histories and funding mechanisms mean that the implementation of a national policy varies between LAs. There are considerable differences between LAs and schools in terms of who is seen as having special educational needs, and where and how these needs are met (see also Chapter 2). It is, therefore essential to remember these variations when comparing schools and LAs.

In addition many LAs have been working to reduce the numbers of statements of special educational needs that are issued by delegating funds directly to schools through a variety of mechanisms that allocate additional resources to schools through moderated panels or cluster arrangements. One consequence has been that simple comparisons from one school to another, or one LA to another, are likely to be less reliable than the numbers in a database might suggest. Just because a school has a high proportion of children designated as having special educational needs does not make it an inclusive school, nor does a low proportion of such children mean that the school is not inclusive. Thus there are difficulties with how the variables within the dataset should be interpreted.

The arbitrary way in which some children become defined as having special educational needs, together with the loose nature of definitions, has restricted the development of accountability systems for such children. Historically, the system had very poor data about patterns of identification and provision for children in the mainstream (McLaughlin *et al.*, 2006). Until the introduction of the NPD, the English system could only account for the relatively small proportion of children with statements of special education need and children placed in special schools. In spite of its limitations, the NPD now contains data about all children described as having special needs and in 2004 a controversial development in the annual schools census was introduced.

The reintroduction of categories of special needs

In response to the lack of specificity in the special needs data held at national level, the Pupil Level Annual Schools Census (PLASC) was amended in 2004 to include the 11 categories currently used by Ofsted (see Box 3.1). When completing the census forms, schools are now asked to list children according to their primary area of difficulty. In theory, this should provide greater detail about incidence and distribution of different forms of identified special educational needs and patterns of provision may become more clearly identifiable, within and across schools. For example, rather than describing one school as being 'more inclusive' than another (because of the number of students designated as having special needs as a proportion of the number of students on the roll), the PLASC will, it is claimed, be able to identify which schools are most able to include which 'types' of special educational needs as well as being able to identify gaps and anomalies in provision.

However, the census forms are completed by different people in different schools who have very different understandings of the complexities of classifying children. In some cases the task is seen as purely administrative and the census is completed by an administrator; in others the census return is completed after careful professional consideration. Thus, the quality of judgements is variable. Whilst the use of categories will lead to more detailed information, it will not necessarily lead to more accurate information. And, because of the difficulties outlined above, it will not be able to show in a consistent manner which students have which kind of difficulties in different schools.

Consequently, increasing the number of categories is likely to lead to more data but to less consistency. Such a system will inevitably be subject to inaccuracy and over-simplification in ways that other categories used in PLASC, such as age and gender, are not. As Florian *et al.* (2004: 117) point out:

A student who is female and aged 12–13 continues to be female and aged 12–13 for the course of a school year. If her family circumstances change and she becomes eligible for free school meals then that change is a precise one (she either is or is not eligible to receive free school meals, even if the

Box 3.1   Categories of special educational needs (based on *Code of Practice* and Ofsted)

A. Cognitive and learning
Specific Learning Disability (SpLD)
Moderate Learning Difficulty (MLD)
Severe Learning Difficulty (SLD)
Profound and Multiple Learning Difficulty (PMLD)
B. Social, emotional and behavioural
Social, Emotional and Behavioural Difficulty (SEBD)
C. Communication and interaction
Speech, Language and Communication Needs (SLCN)
Autism Spectrum Disorder (ASD)
D. Sensory and/or physical
Hearing Impairment (HI)
Visual Impairment (VI)
Multi-Sensory Impairment (MSI)
Physical Difficulty (PD)
Other (OTH)

---

circumstances leading to the change may differ from student to student). Any errors in these aspects of the data are likely to be caused by introducing an error at the point of entering the data, rather than the fundamental difficulties arising from imprecise categories and faulty judgements based on a lack of understanding.

Categories of special educational needs cannot be easily determined when definitions are so imprecise: children change, difficulties come and go, and categories are open to interpretation and are context specific. Some of these difficulties are already apparent in the document, *Data Collection by Type of Special Educational Needs* (DfES, 2003b: 118), which states: 'We are asking for pupils' greatest/primary and secondary needs'. Therefore, allocating individual students and groups of students on the basis of their identified special educational needs will not be straightforward and comparisons of these groups will be problematic. Attempts to produce greater specificity about the nature of children's needs may lull people into believing that the categories are real. Classifying students by 'types' of special educational needs may be considered regressive (Florian *et al.*, 2004) because doing so may:

- increase inappropriate labelling;
- lead to a situation where labels become part of a child's identity;
- ignore recent developments in new international classification systems such as the International Classification of Functioning (ICF) that challenge traditional ways of thinking about categories and labels;

- lead people to believe that different 'kinds' of children need different kinds of provision;
- return to deficit notions of disability by promoting the notion that the 'fault' is in the student rather than encouraging people to examine the learning context;
- ignore the interactive and contextual aspects of teaching and learning;
- oversimplify the complexity of children's difficulties by having to identify a primary type and cause of special educational need; and
- lower teachers' and parents' expectations.

Although some might argue that the (re)introduction of such categories may help and even reassure adults by providing a 'reason' for a child's difficulty, it may also inhibit flexible and interactive approaches to support the participation and learning of all students in schools. Medical categories and their associated labels encourage a focus on the present failure rather than on future possibilities and potential achievements. Further it is likely to increase the number of children who are incorrectly classified, in part because the guidance to schools on how to allocate children is vague, the categories are imprecise, and the process often relies on one person's judgements. Finally, categories of special educational needs imply nominal level data from which comparisons between classes cannot be made. However, levels in the *Code of Practice* may be ranked so that ordinal comparisons can be made even though one may not be comparing like with like.

Nature of attainment data in the NPD

It is beyond the scope of this chapter to explore all the variables in the NPD and the PLASC; however, some comments on the nature of the attainment data are necessary. Any evaluation of the achievement of students will depend on a set of outcome measures against which individuals can be assessed. In recent years in England these have focused on measures against which schools can be held accountable. A crucial question is whether existing approaches to assessment, in particular the Key Stage tests (commonly called Standard Assessment Tests or SATS) plus GCSEs/GNVQs, are capable of demonstrating the progress of all individuals over time. In this regard there are still unanswered questions: whose learning is of importance (all/some children)? What outcomes should be assessed? And, how will they be assessed? Under the current system there are significant numbers of children identified as having special educational needs for whom the current SATS and GCSEs/GNVQs provide no meaningful data.

In an attempt to rectify this issue, P-scales (DfES, 2006) have been introduced for children who have not reached level one of the national curriculum. It is unclear whether these data can be meaningfully used to compare performance of an individual over time, let alone at the school level. Though P-scales are a differentiated outcome for students who may not be expected to perform at normative levels within each Key Stage, they are also a component of the desire for a unified system of accountability that includes all learners and an attempt to provide access to a common curriculum and assessment system for all children. Nevertheless, early evidence of their use suggests that they are helpful in the planning process and have provided teachers and schools with the means for recognising and recording progress for those children and young people for whom level one of the national curriculum is unobtainable at the time of assessment. The development of a common set of outcome measures is to be welcomed and it may help in the construction of value-added measures for students identified as having special educational needs that will have national currency. However, progress on the implementation of P-scales has not been easy. Thus the data contained in the NPD may not be capable of showing the progress of some students because the national tests do not produce data that are helpful in this regard.

The extent to which a common set of outcome indicators is desirable is only one aspect of this issue. Just as important is the extent to which a common set of assessment and testing techniques and approaches is technically feasible. The debate about test or examination adaptations, sometimes referred to as accommodations, centres around whether changing tests to make them more accessible means that simple comparisons of performance become untenable. As yet there is little evidence about whether accommodations, such as extra time, allowing alternative responses or having a reader, invalidate the results of such tests (Rouse *et al.*, 2000). Further, as more low-achieving students are included in national assessments, questions have been raised in a recent EPPI review about the negative impact of such testing on students' motivation and self-esteem (Harlen and Crick, 2002). The problematic issues related to the assessment of students designated as having special educational needs are central to the debate about inclusion and school effectiveness. The desire to construct a dataset that includes all children's achievements might be seen as a worthwhile aspiration but it does not make it technically feasible.

How reliable and valid are achievement data?

There are a number of reasons why the results from the national tests taken at the end of each Key Stage of education may not be particularly valid and reliable. Difficulties with validity include questions about the extent to which the tests actually test the relevant skills and knowledge of that area of the curriculum. Questions of reliability concern the technical adequacy of the tests, the extent to which they are sufficiently sensitive to demonstrate learning for all children, and whether any adaptations or amendments made for students thought to have special needs undermine reliability. But perhaps most important of all when it comes to answering questions about inclusion and achievement is whether a national system of assessment can include all children in a meaningful way.

Some of these difficulties are brought into stark focus when comparisons are made between performance at the end of Key Stage 2 and the end of Key Stage 3. A cursory review of the data indicates that a significant number of students do not improve their national curriculum level scores between KS2 and KS3. There are several possible explanations:

- These students do not make measurable progress in the first three years of secondary school (Years 7, 8 and 9)
- The national curriculum levels are too imprecise and/or broad to reflect precisely the learning that has occurred
- The KS2 assessments are too generous
- The KS3 assessments are too harsh
- KS2 and KS3 level tests are not comparable
- Some primary schools are targeting borderline grade students to boost their performance from level three to level four in the KS2 tests
- Some secondary schools pay little attention to KS3 attainment, concentrating instead on GCSE/GNVQ at the end of KS4.

Completeness

Although the PLASC and NPD aim to be comprehensive, they contain a number of omissions and errors. First, they can only be as reliable as the data provided by the schools. Errors relating to the ethnicity, mother tongue or special needs designation of students are difficult to identify. Further, there are relatively large numbers of students for whom there are missing assessment data, especially students who experience difficulties in learning. This can partly be explained by mobility and migration, but also by official and unofficial ways in which certain students do not get to take the tests. It may also be a function of exclusion in its various forms. Such missing data make it difficult to answer questions about the achievement of students identified as having special educational needs.

Which data to use?

Two main types of data are crucial here: measures of achievement, and measures of inclusion. However, both are problematic and need to be treated with caution.

In devising a system that enables individual progress over time to be demonstrated, some crucial decisions have to be made about how to treat the data. For instance, at GCSE/GNVQ, given that there is considerable range and variation of GCSEs and GNVQs taken between schools, which measure is the most meaningful? The best eight results (known as the capped score), the total points score, average points score, or the number of passes at A* to C? Also, decisions have to be made about which data are used for baseline purposes. The most commonly used achievement data are scores from Key Stage tests which are then compared with tests taken subsequently, but these scores are not directly comparable though they are often treated as such. These data are also very 'blunt' and are further complicated by unreliability. Moreover, not all children are included in national tests and examinations. Crucially, it is often the students at risk of exclusion for whom there are missing data. The limitations of national achievement data are considered in more detail elsewhere in this book and whilst it is acknowledged that achievement is difficult to measure, at least there are some data to consider.

Meanwhile, measures of inclusion are even more complex and contested. As noted above, having a high proportion of students designated as having special educational needs in a school is not necessarily a measure of inclusion though it has been used as such. In research commissioned by the DfES, Dyson, *et al.* (2004) used the proportion of students who had been placed on their school's special needs register at School Action Plus and those who were the subjects of statements of special educational needs as their measure of 'inclusivity'. They then looked at the academic performance of schools, in terms of national test results, through the NPD with the intention of examining whether school performance was affected, either positively or negatively, by the proportion of students identified as having special educational needs.

Their results indicate that generally there is little or no relationship between inclusion and achievement (using their definitions of inclusivity and achievement), and they argue that at 'school level, inclusivity does not determine performance' (p.49). Furthermore, their research has led them to suggest that: 'There may be something to learn from schools which manage to reconcile high levels of inclusivity with high levels of attainment' (ibid.). That is, research should consider the policies and practices of individual schools that support the inclusion of a diverse range of students, so as to examine the effects of those policies and practices on the achievements of all students in the school and not only those who have been identified as having special educational needs.

As Dyson and his colleagues recognise, calculating the proportion of students in a school who have been identified as having special educational needs says little about how far and in what ways that school is, or is not, inclusive. First, as we have already noted, there are significant variations between LAs and schools in terms of who is identified as having special educational needs. In their research report on the progress of the 2001 Education Act (SENDA), Ofsted (2004: 10) notes: 'The inconsistency with which pupils are defined as having SEN is a continuing concern'. Second, information about the physical presence of students designated as having special educational needs in a school does not explain how far policies and practices support their inclusion in the life of that school. Third, using data from the NPD and the PLASC to examine the progress of such students, let alone across whole student cohorts in a school, is not straightforward. Findings from the Ofsted report also note that: 'Gathering reliable data about the progress of pupils with SEN continues to prove problematic for schools and LEAs, with uncertainty in schools about what constitutes adequate progress. Use of comparative data is weak'. Finally, as Slee (2005) has shown, identification of special needs is in itself a form of exclusion, and therefore cannot be used as a proxy measure of inclusion.

With this in mind, we have conducted research to explore whether schools with higher proportions of students designated as having special educational needs performed differently from schools with lower proportions, without making assumptions about the inclusive nature of their policies and practices (Rouse and Florian, 2006). Our research was designed to investigate whether the admission of such students into mainstream secondary schools negatively affects the achievements of other students. By combining selected variables from the NPD on student achievement with PLASC data on special educational needs, we examined the progress of one cohort of students from one local authority across the five years of their secondary schooling. Progress of students from three secondary schools where there are higher proportions of students identified with special educational needs (25 per cent) was compared with the progress of students from the same cohort in all schools across the LA. Comparisons were made with the progress of students in similar schools (co-educational comprehensive schools) and also with the progress of students in schools where the proportion of students identified with special educational needs is lower (12 per cent). To explore whether there were variations in achievement between the schools, attainment on entry to secondary school was compared with subsequent GCSE/GNVQ performance, both for those students who had been identified as having special educational needs and for those who had not, so that the notion of 'progress' over the five years of secondary schooling could be considered. A simple 'value-added' measure of individual progress over the five years of secondary schooling was developed by dividing capped GCSE/GNVQ point scores by Key Stage 2 average point scores to produce a 'coefficient of progress'.

Comparison of group means for the three types of school showed progress in the schools with a higher proportion of students identified as having special educational needs to be greater than the mean progress in the comparison schools. To explore further the finding that these schools seem to perform better than schools where the proportion of such students is lower, we compared each one of them against the comparison schools. Here a more complex picture of the three schools emerged. Performance in one was similar to performance in the comparison schools, while in another the performance was considerably higher, but in the third school it was somewhat lower.

Because schools with large numbers of children described as having special educational needs are not necessarily inclusive schools, it is important to supplement any quantitative analysis with qualitative measures in order to explore the 'stories' behind the numbers, as we do in the next section of this book. This is also necessary because the designation of special educational need in England is based in part on the organisational response put in place to meet students' identified needs and thus can confound any quantification of special educational needs that is used in the national database.

In this chapter we have attempted to explore some of the conceptual and technical issues in using the newly available national datasets in England to answer questions about inclusion and achievement. Notably, the definition of special educational needs, differences in patterns of provision across LAs, and the variable number of children who could be described as having special educational needs make it difficult to collect or meaningfully analyse statistics about provision, attainment or the students. However, there is some value in looking at trends as long as the data are used and interpreted cautiously. Because of the enormous scale and the structure of the NPD and the PLASC, the data they contain may be assigned meanings that they do not hold. That is, they may become 'the' instrument by which students and schools are measured, rather than 'a' lens through which some understanding may be reached. Information that is not available through the NPD or PLASC may be ignored or given less status and the information in the datasets may be inaccurate.

The sheer scale of the available dataset is one of its strengths, allowing larger and more comprehensive samples of students, schools, or LAs to be considered. The advantage of the PLASC dataset over other census and survey databases is that the PLASC is a dataset of the whole population (with certain exceptions) rather than a sample from within it. This eliminates problems associated with working with incomplete or partial samples as well as the dilemma of accounting for low participant response rates.

However, there are risks in using large, complete samples. Researchers may be more inclined to declare statistical significance in their findings given that they may be unrestrained by the limitations of working with a representative sample of the population. Additionally, statistical analyses that have very large denominators (sample size) are more likely to show statistical significance even where there is no educational significance. Reports of significance using large sample sizes must be interpreted with caution. Ironically, a large dataset can introduce errors of bias just as with a small sample through overconfidence in findings and a greater likelihood of demonstrating unimportant statistical associations.

Further, researchers may be tempted to assume that the data contained in the NPD and PLASC are accurate. Although the DfES is taking great care in the construction of the dataset, they recognise that errors and omissions exist, including some students having been assigned to the wrong national curriculum year group. Moreover, it must be remembered that there are incomplete records for some students, including those who are working below level one of the national curriculum, and those who are highly mobile. So whilst the NPD should include all children and young people, there are some who are currently not included in the 'population'.

Nevertheless, the NPD and PLASC provide practitioners and researchers with an unprecedented opportunity to consider educational performance indicators in relation to various student characteristics such as socio-economic status (SES) through eligibility for free school meals (FSM) or home post code, special needs status, behaviour (as implied through exclusion), ethnicity, mother tongue, month of birth and mobility. Clearly these data have value at the national, local and school level. In justifying the collection of data about types of special needs the DfES (2003b: 1) state that:

> In order to help planning and policy development, we need more information about the numbers of pupils in the country with different types of special educational need (SEN) ... The data will be used to help planning, to study trends and to monitor the outcomes of initiatives and interventions on pupils with different types of SEN.

The statement above contains a number of assumptions about what such data can tell us; what it does not do is to consider the problems or limitations of making these assumptions.

Assessing inclusivity

Although some research (for example, Dyson *et al*., 2004) has used the proportion of students identified as having special educational needs as an indicator of a school's 'inclusivity', admitting a high proportion of such children does not mean that a school is necessarily inclusive. The NPD provides information about how many such children the school claims to have and it now also contains information about the children's primary needs, but these data tell us nothing about inclusive practices and levels of participation in the school. As discussed in Chapter 2, the concept of inclusion is not straightforward and there are numerous ways of understanding inclusive education. One approach might be to take a school improvement perspective, focusing on the expansion of a school's capacity to respond to all its students. Another approach might be described as a 'special education approach' in which the students, staff, expertise, resources and facilities previously located in special schools are relocated in what are sometimes called additionally resourced mainstream schools. In addition, special services and schools may be reconfigured in ways that connect them to one or a number of mainstream schools, for example through dual placements or outreach support.

In practice, a relatively high or low proportion of students designated as having special educational needs within a particular school may be as much a function of historical patterns of provision and resourcing, as it is a consequence of inclusion policy, or indeed, inclusive practice. Thus numbers of such students within a school tell us very little about inclusive practices or levels of participation: to assume that a higher proportion equates with inclusion is to make a fundamental error in the research or policy analysis process.

Conclusion

In spite of the limitations outlined above, questions about inclusion and achievement can start to be addressed by interrogating the national data and they provide an important resource in helping with this crucial task. However, it is necessary to be aware of what the data can and cannot tell us. The ways in which the variables are selected and used are crucial here. It is important to develop robust understandings of value-added and also to be clear about how inclusive schools are not necessarily those that have high numbers of children designated as having special educational needs. If these complex and contested concepts are to be understood more fully, then it is necessary to go beyond the numbers and to carry out in-depth studies of inclusive practices in schools where the data were produced. Approaches such as those promoted by *Leading on Inclusion* (DfES, 2005b) are a useful start, but they could be improved by acknowledging the problematic nature of these concepts and by encouraging schools to be more questioning about their recommended strategies. Meaningful answers to questions about inclusion and achievement may be found, but they require the systematic collection and analysis of extensive qualitative data as well as a careful scrutiny and a healthy understanding of the limitations of the national pupil database.

4   Examining the relationship between inclusion and achievement

The Framework for Participation

> I am all for inclusion but when a child arrives with high levels of need my heart sinks ... because we don't have the resources to support them and because of the effect on the SATs results.
>
> (Headteacher comment, Audit Commission, 2002: 49)

In Chapter 1 we reviewed how, over the last two decades, there has been a disjunction in national educational policies in England. On the one hand, legislation for special education has become increasingly enabling, inclusive and progressive, whilst on the other hand, raising the achievement of all children, as part of an ongoing standards agenda, continues to dominate educational debate (Florian *et al.*, 2004). The relationship and tensions between the inclusion of some children and the achievement of all have contributed to an enduring and widespread perception amongst some policy makers and practitioners (as noted in the headteacher's comment above) that certain groups of children, and in particular those whose behaviour is more troubling and troubled, have a detrimental effect on the achievement of all other children. However, as we pointed out in Chapter 1, high levels of inclusion can be entirely compatible with high levels of achievement. Indeed, we concur with Mittler (1999: vii) who argues that the debate on inclusion must also be 'about human rights and about the kind of society and the kinds of schools we want for all our children'. Combining inclusion with high levels of achievement is not only possible but essential if all children are to have the opportunity to participate fully in education.

In Chapter 2 we examined the range of ways in which the inclusion and the achievement of children and young people in schools is understood by practitioners, policy makers and academics. We argued that a more nuanced interpretation of either concept requires a stronger recognition of the relationship between them. In Chapter 3 we added to this debate by considering the problems and possibilities for researching inclusion through the use of national datasets of student achievement and other demographic data. We suggested that a multi-method approach, that combines national data with school-level case studies, can be a particularly useful and robust means of understanding the relationship between inclusion and achievement. This reasoning has shaped our own research which we present in the following four chapters, each of which comprises a multi-method case study of a single school.

The purpose of this chapter is to describe the *Framework for Participation*, which is the research tool, or methodological lens, with which these four case studies were constructed. The *Framework* helped to shape our decisions about interviews (who to interview, what to ask), observations (who to see, where, what to record), documentary/archival sources (what to collect) and statistical data (what to use). It allowed us to scrutinise the policies, practices and everyday interactions that make up the life of any school, and, in doing so, to explore the key themes and concerns raised in earlier chapters of this book. In particular, we wanted to examine how inclusion and achievement, and related concepts ('special educational needs', 'learning difficulties', 'disabilities', 'standards', 'attainment', 'progress', 'aptitudes', etc.) were understood and used by a range of members within a school and the consequences of those different meanings and applications. Thus we were interested in members' underlying beliefs about notions such as 'same' and 'different', and 'normal' and 'other' (Florian, 2007).

The *Framework* also supported our research intention to consider how these issues interacted at different levels within a school: that is, to understand the educational experiences of not only an individual child or young person but also a particular group of students or a classroom, as well as across a whole school and beyond, taking into account local and national influences and concerns. Thus the *Framework* is concerned with the participation of all members of a school, including students, teachers, support staff and parents/carers. It sets out to understand why one school may be more successful than another, often similar school at supporting both the inclusion and achievement of its members. We were concerned to explore the underlying values and beliefs embedded in the cultures of a school and to identify existing and potential strategies to raise achievement and inclusion and, thereby, to enable that school to become increasingly participatory. (For background to the development of the *Framework*, see Black-Hawkins, 2002.)

What is participation?

This section outlines the conceptualisation of participation on which the *Framework* is based. We have used this term as a way of bringing together, understanding and re-defining inclusion and achievement. Box 4.1 provides a summary of the principal elements of participation. However, the following definition by Booth (2002: 2) offers a most useful starting point:

> Participation in education involves going beyond access. It implies learning alongside others and collaborating with them in shared lessons. It involves active engagement with what is learnt and taught, and having a say in how education is experienced. But participation also involves being recognised for oneself and being accepted for oneself. I participate with you, when you recognise me as a person like yourself, and accept me for who I am.

Box 4.1   Principal elements of participation

- Impacts upon all members of a school and all aspects of school life
- Comprises two interconnected and never-ending processes
- Concerned with responses to diversity
- Distanced conceptually from notions of 'special educational needs'
- Requires learning to be active and collaborative for all
- Necessitates the active right of members to 'join in'
- Based on relationships of mutual recognition and acceptance

Impacts upon all members of a school and all aspects of school life

Participation, because it concerns both achievement and inclusion, necessarily relates to the experiences of *all* members of a school: staff and parents/carers, as well as students. It does not therefore only apply to a specific group, or groups, of students categorised as having 'special educational needs'. Indeed, using this term to describe students may act as a barrier to their participation (Booth *et al.*, 2000). Similarly, participation is also concerned with *all* aspects of the life of a school and not just the teaching and learning which occur in classrooms, although this too is important. It relates to a school's formal policies and practices as well as the countless everyday interactions that take place amongst its members.

Comprises two interconnected and never-ending processes

To make sense of participation it is necessary to understand its close relationship to barriers to participation: increasing participation reduces barriers to participation and vice versa. However, these processes are not always easy to identify. They can be complex, ambiguous and opaque. Activities in a school may increase participation for some whilst reinforcing barriers to participation for others. These interconnected and never-ending processes are constantly shifting and may be difficult to change (Ballard, 1995). There can be no such institution as a 'fully participatory' one: but it is an aspiration well worth pursuing.

Concerned with responses to diversity

Participation is concerned with responses to diversity within a school. These include understandings of, and attitudes towards, ethnicity (e.g. Riehl, 2000; Blair and Bourne, 1998), gender (e.g. Riddell, 1992; Siraj-Blatchford, 1993; Blyth and Milner, 1997), disability (e.g. Oliver, 1990; Thomas *et al.*, 1998) and ability (Hart *et al.*, 2004). As demonstrated in all these texts, discrimination is often subtle and complex, sometimes unintended, and rarely straightforward; see, for example, Gillborn and Youdell's (2000) exploration of the interplay between poverty, class, ethnicity and gender in the educational experiences of students. However, the devaluation of any member of a school, for whatever reasons, forms a barrier to their participation. This is not to suggest that all students receive identical learning experiences but rather that their diversity is recognised and used 'as a rich resource to support the learning of all' (Booth *et al.*, 2000: 12).

Distanced conceptually from notions of 'special educational needs'

However well we define a word, the ways in which it is understood by others is also partly determined by how they choose to use it themselves. This is not just a matter of wordplay. The concept of inclusion continues to be shaped by past interpretations and in particular their association with the notion of the physical presence and absence of students in mainstream schools. Even in some texts which set out to argue for a wider whole-school interpretation of inclusion, there remains an enduring focus on specific groups of students who are considered to have learning difficulties (Sebba, 1997; Thomas *et al.*, 1998; Corbett, 1999). The concept of participation does not carry this burden of the past and in particular it is distanced from the notion of 'special educational needs'. Although participation is, rightly, concerned with physical access to and within schools, this is only one aspect of a much broader understanding of schools and education which encompasses all students and staff engaging in activities inside and outside classrooms.

Requires learning to be active and collaborative for all

Participation requires the active and collaborative learning of students, in which they make choices about what they learn as well as how they work together to support each other's learning; that is, being 'actively involved' (Hopkins *et al.*, 1997). This is not, therefore, about 'special' provision for 'special' students who are considered to have learning difficulties. To paraphrase the title of Hart's (1996) book, it is about the enhancement of all students' learning 'through innovative thinking', that is, using available resources, including students and other staff, in creative ways. This understanding of participatory learning can also be extended to include members of staff participating in active and collaborative learning with their colleagues and therefore working towards what Southworth (1994) terms a 'learning school'. The contribution of all teaching and non-teaching staff, as well as students and parents/carers, should be recognised and differences acknowledged, encouraged and welcomed because they provide a range of experiences, understanding and interests that make up the membership of a school.

Necessitates the active right of members to 'join in'

Inclusion suggests a passivity on the part of members of a school, whereas participation stresses the notion of actively 'joining in'. With the former, therefore, there is a sense of the conditional: members are allowed, even perhaps encouraged, by others to be included. For the latter, participation is a right that is shared by all. However, this in turn also implies reciprocal responsibilities; that is, there is a right and a responsibility to participate in learning alongside and with others, as well as a right and a responsibility to participate in decision-making processes; see also Macmurray (1950), below.

Based on relationships of mutual recognition and acceptance

There are useful parallels between the concept of participation and Fielding's understanding of the nature of 'schools as communities' (1998, 1999) and 'person-centred' schools (2000). In both the quality of relationships between members of a school is paramount. Fielding draws on the work of the philosopher Macmurray who argued that relationships should be based on the two fundamental principles of freedom and equality.

> If we do not treat one another as equals, we exclude freedom from the relationship. Freedom too, conditions equality. For if there is restraint between us there is fear; and to counter the fear we must seek control over its object, and attempt to subordinate the other person to our own power. Any attempt to achieve freedom without equality, or to achieve equality without freedom, must, therefore be self-defeating.
>
> (Macmurray, 1950: 74)

This emphasis on 'freedom' and 'equality' also relates to the rights and responsibilities noted earlier. That is, members have the right to be themselves whilst accepting the responsibility for valuing other members as their equals. Macmurray, however, does not define equality in terms of assimilation, stating: 'It is precisely the recognition of difference and variety amongst individuals that gives meaning to the assertion of equality' (1938: 4). All relationships in schools require recognition and acceptance: those between students and staff as well as those amongst students and amongst staff. And, they are enacted not only through policies and practices, but also in the countless informal personal interactions that take place amongst students and staff in any school.

Purposes of the *Framework for Participation*

The primary purposes of the *Framework* are outlined in the introduction to this chapter. A summary is provided in Box 4.2.

Not only are all five purposes closely connected but they can lead to what appears to be contradictory findings. Certain policies or practices may promote greater participation for some members of a school whilst at the same time reinforce barriers to participation for others. Indeed, the impact of some policies and practices even on individual members may be ambivalent. Such instances are explored in the case study chapters, later in the book. One prevalent example is the practice of withdrawing students with low literacy levels from mainstream

Box 4.2   The *Framework for Participation* sets out to ...

- examine the participation of all members of a school: students, teaching and non-teaching staff and parents/carers.
- explore the complexities of the educational experiences of individual and groups of children and young people and staff, as well as across whole classes, schools and beyond.
- address why some schools are more successful than other similar schools at supporting both the inclusion and achievement of students and staff.
- scrutinise a school's policies and practices and everyday interactions so as to reveal the underlying values and beliefs embedded in its cultures.
- identify existing and potential strategies which are effective in raising achievement and inclusion, as well as those which may reduce barriers to achievement and inclusion.

---

lessons so as to provide small-group intensive teaching in reading and writing. Such provision arguably both supports and impedes their participation. On the one hand, improved literacy competence will allow such students greater access to the curriculum in the future; on the other hand, withdrawal excludes them from the current learning experiences of their peers in mainstream classes. Clark *et al.* (1999) describe this as the 'commonality-difference dilemma' (p.171). They argue that if staff respond to students' diversity they 'ipso facto create different forms of provision for different students and thus become less than fully inclusive'. Yet, if staff ignore students' diversity they may exclude them from participation by 'offering them experiences from which they [are] alienated' (p.172).

The intention of the *Framework* is not to smooth away the everyday complexities of schools, but to provide a means by which they can be more clearly understood. In such cases, it is perhaps the values and beliefs underlying the decisions behind policies and practices that require most careful consideration.

Structuring the *Framework for Participation*

The *Framework* is divided into three main sections, as summarised in Box 4.3. These provide the overall structure by which the principal elements of participation, as discussed above, are considered. Each section relates to an aspect of what it means to participate, or not to participate, fully in the life of a school.

These sections are supplemented by a series of questions (see Box 4.4) intended to initiate an examination of the processes of participation and barriers to participation. In many ways it is the 'why' questions that are most pertinent in understanding participation, for in addressing these, the reasons and purposes underlying 'who' and 'what' are more easily revealed. However, to make sense

Box 4.3   Sections of the *Framework for Participation*

---

1   Participation and ACCESS: being there
2   Participation and COLLABORATION: learning together
3   Participation and DIVERSITY: recognition and acceptance.

Box 4.4   'Who?', 'What?' and 'Why?' of participation

- Who does and does not participate? And, who decides this?
- What are the policies, practices and interactions that promote participation in the school? What are the policies, practices and interactions that strengthen barriers to participation?
- Why do these processes of participation exist within the cultures (values and beliefs) of the school? Why do these barriers to participation exist within the cultures (values and beliefs) of the school?

---

of 'why' necessitates an exploration of the underlying values and beliefs which shape the cultures and thus the policies and practices and everyday interactions of a school. Such scrutiny can prove to be a difficult and challenging task, but without doing so, efforts to become more participatory may be superficial.

The next stage of the *Framework* is shown in Box 4.5. Here each of the three main sections has been sub-divided into a number of related elements, and accompanied by a series of questions based on the ones noted above. Of course, in the everyday reality of any school the three main sections which structure the *Framework for Participation* are not experienced by its members as discrete entities. Therefore decisions about where to include specific aspects of participation may, at times, seem arbitrary. Participation and Diversity, in particular, permeates all policies and practices in a school. For example, decisions about *Access* and admissions are partly based on understandings of and attitudes towards student diversity. Similarly, successful *Collaboration* is, to some extent, dependent upon members acknowledging that the range of experiences and expertise amongst them is a resource that may enrich the learning of students and staff, rather than simply a problem to be overcome. Finally, of the three main sections, that of Participation and Diversity is also the most problematic in terms of identifying processes of and barriers to participation. This is not only to do with its pervasiveness, but also because the values and beliefs which underpin relationships between members of a school are often covert and unquestioned by staff and students alike.

Chapter 10 offers structured guidance to support practitioners who wish to explore participation by examining the relationship between inclusion and achievement in schools. It provides a comprehensive set of ideas to support the

Box 4.5   Elements and questions of the *Framework for Participation*

---

1   Participation and ACCESS: being there
–   Joining the school
–   Staying in the school
–   Access to spaces and places
–   Access to the curriculum
•   Who is given access and by whom? Who is denied access and by whom?
•   What are the policies, practices and interactions that promote access? What are the policies, practices and interactions that reinforce barriers to access?
•   Why within the cultures (values and beliefs) of the school is greater access afforded to some individuals/groups? And, why is access withheld from some individuals/groups?
2   Participation and COLLABORATION: learning together
–   Learning alongside other students
–   Supporting students to learn together
–   Members of staff working together
–   Schools and other institutions working together
•   Who learns together? Who does not learn together?
•   What are the policies, practices and interactions that promote collaboration? What are the policies, practices and interactions that reinforce barriers to collaboration?
•   Why within the cultures (values and beliefs) of the school do some individuals/groups learn together? And, why are there barriers to some individuals/groups learning together?
3   Participation and DIVERSITY: recognition and acceptance
–   Recognition and acceptance of students, by staff
–   Recognition and acceptance of staff, by staff
–   Recognition and acceptance of students, by students
•   Who is recognised and accepted as a person and by whom? Who is not recognised and accepted as a person and by whom?
•   What are the policies, practices and interactions that promote recognition and acceptance? What are the policies, practices and interactions that form barriers to recognition and acceptance?
•   Why within the cultures (values and beliefs) of the school are some individuals/groups recognised and accepted? And, why are there barriers to the recognition and acceptance of some individuals/groups?

collection of evidence for each of the *Framework*'s three main sections and their further sub-divisions. This includes suggestions about interviews, observations, documentary/archival sources and statistical data. All of these make use of evidence that is readily available in schools. In the next four chapters, we present our four case studies so as to illustrate some of the ways in which the *Framework* may be used as a means of questioning, researching and understanding participation – inclusion and achievement – in schools.

Part II

The case studies

Part II comprises four chapters, each of which is a case study of a school, two primary and two secondary, all situated in the same urban local authority. When selecting the schools we asked LA staff for suggestions based on the following criteria: first, that the schools enrolled a diverse student population from their local communities and second, that they were all approaching the task of becoming more inclusive and raising achievement but in a variety of different ways. Applying these criteria was not straightforward because, as discussed in previous chapters, the concepts of inclusion and achievement are open to a range of interpretations. Nevertheless, four schools were chosen. They were not necessarily the highest achieving schools in the LA as measured by end of Key Stage test results, rather they were schools which the LA staff believed were grappling with ways to improve achievement within the context of maintaining a highly inclusive student intake. We did not choose schools that applied any form of student selection, such as single sex and/or faith-based schools.

Purposes of the case study chapters

The primary purpose of the case studies is to provide readers with a detailed examination of the complex relationship between students' inclusion and achievement through stories about real schools. Whilst all four schools share certain characteristics, as noted above, the policies and practices which they have developed to support the inclusion and achievement of their students varies tremendously across and within each of the schools. Therefore another important purpose of the case studies is to illustrate the wide range of approaches that different practitioners have adopted at the level of the school and the classroom and for individual students. Each school has particular priorities, challenges and resources and the case studies set out to reveal and celebrate this variability. Finally, the case studies are intended to support readers in identifying ways of understanding, monitoring and developing students' achievement and inclusion in their own schools and classrooms.

Undertaking the case studies

We used the *Framework for Participation*, as set out in the previous chapter, as guidance to gather, present and discuss our findings for each case study. We visited the schools, in pairs, over the course of two terms, spending the equivalent of approximately eight days in each school. During that time we observed staff, students and other members of the school communities at work and play: in classrooms, staffrooms, playgrounds, corridors, meetings, assemblies and canteens. We interviewed formally a range of staff as well as talked more informally to children and other adults. We also collected documents relating to policies and practices in each of the schools. Decisions about who to interview, who/what to observe and which documents to collect were partly guided by the circumstances of individual schools. Finally, we drew on available evidence from national datasets. The names of the schools and their members have been changed to protect confidentiality and maintain anonymity. Throughout all our visits to the schools we were always made welcome.

Some background to provision in the local authority

At the time of our research there were 66 primary and 16 secondary schools in the LA, with a total enrolment of approximately 28,000 primary aged children and 17,000 secondary aged students. For more than a decade, the LA has been seeking alternative strategies to special school placements such as the development of resourced provision in mainstream schools. These schools were provided with additional funding to enable them to offer appropriate support such as specialist staff, resources and facilities to groups of students identified as having special educational needs who, in the past, might otherwise have been offered special school places. More recently, the LA has moved towards models of support, development and training that encourage all mainstream schools to develop their own capacity to accommodate and take responsibility for including all students. All four case studies reflect this broader diversity of student intake.

Ofsted (2005a) points out that the local authority's special educational needs provision is very good, with a long-standing commitment to inclusion in terms of the high levels of placement within mainstream settings. Furhermore, the authority not only has a low proportion of children attending special schools, but it is also one of the fastest improving authorities and has one of the highest 'value added' scores in the country. Whilst performance of younger age groups compares least favourably with other LAs, demographic factors such as children not speaking English when they arrive at school and high student mobility mean that it is necessary to exercise caution in using the figures as an indicator of the quality of provision in primary schools. According to Ofsted (2005a):

> Pupil performance in schools improves in relation to other local authorities as children get older. At KS4 performance is particularly strong in terms of the low proportion of pupils who leave school without any qualifications. Rates

of improvement in recent years have been better than the national average in almost all respects in Key Stages two, three and four.

In addition, Ofsted (2005a) also points out that the authority serves its most vulnerable children well, with a significantly higher proportion of 'looked after' children achieving 5+ A*–C grades at GCSE than the national average. Table II.1 provides a snapshot of comparative point scores for 2005. It shows clearly the progress made at KS4.

Table II.1   Snapshot of LA Key Stage scores for 2005 (DfES website)

Key Stage Average Point Scores	England	Local Authority	Range for Individual Schools in LA
KS2	27.6	26.9	24.4 – 28.6
KS3	34.5	32.2	29.1 – 36.0
KS4: GCSE/equivalent	355.2	354.7	263.4 – 498.7

5 Kingsley Primary School

Introducing Kingsley Primary School

Kingsley Primary is a co-educational community school for children aged three to eleven. It is a relatively large primary school of three-form entry, with a single nursery class. When we visited there were approximately 650 children on roll. Separate infants and junior schools were established on a shared site in the 1950s, but in 1998 they were amalgamated into one school. Many of the original buildings remain in use although more recently a large-scale building improvement, budgeted at about £1.5 million, has started.

The school faces a number of challenging circumstances. There is a high level of mobility amongst families moving in and out of the local area. The school's most recent Ofsted report (February, 2002) recorded that, over the course of the previous year, 118 children (21 per cent) had joined the school and 68 children (12 per cent) had transferred elsewhere. Ofsted also noted that three-quarters of the children were from ethnic minority backgrounds, of whom 70 were refugees, and that about 60 per cent of the children spoke English as an additional language. In 2002 just over half of Kingsley's children were eligible for free school meals: well above the then national average of 18 per cent and more than the LA average of 40 per cent. In the same year there were 95 children (14.9 per cent) on the school's special needs register, of whom 4 (0.6 per cent) had been made formally the subject of statements. Both sets of figures were below those at national (22.7 per cent and 1.7 per cent) and LA (18.3 per cent and 1.5 per cent) levels.

In terms of staffing, also in 2002, there were 31 teachers and 18 education support staff (full-time equivalent). Turnover of teachers at Kingsley had been high (over 40 per cent between 2000 and 2002) but has recently been more stable: however, recruitment and retention remains a concern. A new headteacher was appointed in October 2000, to support the school through the Ofsted inspection referred to above, when it was considered to be at serious risk of being placed in special measures. However, under his new leadership this did not happen and Kingsley is now considered to be a highly successful school. In 2002, it was selected by the DfES as one of the 'top one hundred most improved schools' and in 2003 it was awarded a DfES School Achievement Award. Staff who were interviewed referred to the key role played by the headteacher in terms of overall improvement in the school as well as support for them individually.

Examining inclusion and achievement

This section examines the evidence collected from the case study. It is set out according to the main headings from the *Framework for Participation.*

Participation and access: being there

Joining the school

Kingsley's open admission policy is in line with LA arrangements. In practice the school has some spare capacity, with approximately 85 children in a year rather than the 90 it can take. Therefore decisions rarely arise about which children should, and should not, be admitted. In all interviews, staff described the school as having a good reputation locally. Most children from the neighbourhood attend Kingsley but a small number of families opt instead for one of two Church of England schools and, according to the headteacher, not necessarily on religious grounds. He argued that, '[The schools] do not accept behaviour difficulties ... all children wear a uniform ... These contribute to them being seen as successful'. Both schools are over-subscribed and each year approximately 10 to 15 'mainly middle-class' children, who start at Kingsley, transfer when places become available. The headteacher considers this to have a detrimental effect on the school's Key Stage 2 national test results.

The school's prospectus describes Kingsley as 'a fully inclusive school'. This was reiterated by the headteacher: 'We would admit anyone ... although currently not [physically] accessible to all ... we would have found a way'. However, he had reservations about including those children from outside Kingsley's catchment area who had been permanently excluded from other schools. 'The most difficult to integrate are those with behaviour problems ... Not just that individual child's needs but ... [the school] has a responsibility to all children'. Because there are spare places at Kingsley, he argued that the LA put pressure on him to accept such children.

Staff interviewed maintained that they too were in broad agreement with the LA's policy to admit all children to mainstream schools. Some explained that they had had reservations but, through their experiences of working with a wider range of children, their perspectives had shifted. One teacher spoke of a boy who arrived from Egypt with an undiagnosed hearing impairment. After three years he 'has benefited from being in this setting ... socialising ... trying to communicate ... playing'. Another teacher described a girl now in Year 2 who, when she was in reception, had seemed 'neglected ... screamed a lot ... but she's definitely in the right place now ... even though I wasn't sure at the time'.

There was, however, some uncertainty about the inclusion of children with profound and complex learning difficulties regarding lack of resources, especially in terms of staffing and training. Staff referred particularly to one girl in Year 1 who had a severe hearing loss, some visual difficulties, no spoken language (but approximately four British Sign Language signs) and had been identified as being on the autistic spectrum. One LSA (learning support assistant) said, 'If you asked me to say the truth, "Should she be here?" my answer would be, "No" … It seems harder as [she] goes up the years … the gap gets bigger'. Her class teacher was also concerned: 'We're not experts … we do what we can'.

Nonetheless, staff appeared to agree that including such children had a positive effect on the school generally. As one LSA noted: '[It] is very beneficial not just for the child with special needs but for the other children too'. Arguments were based on notions of social justice and a pragmatic understanding that schools should reflect society. One teacher explained: 'It's real life'. Another argued, 'It is not detrimental [to children's learning] … as long as support is provided, and it is, generally, unless the LSA is ill or absent'.

There was one other group of children about whom staff had reservations regarding their inclusion. These were children whose behaviour was considered to be particularly disruptive. Reasons for this were similar to those noted earlier by the headteacher, relating to their damaging effect on others. One teacher explained, they can be 'disturbing for the class … jeopardise the learning of the other children'. Such views provide a contrast to those expressed about children with profound and multiple difficulties, indicating that reflecting some aspects of society is more desirable than others.

Staying in the school

Since the headteacher joined the school in 2000, he has permanently excluded only one child, because of extreme violence towards staff and children. Temporary internal exclusions, however, are built into the school's behaviour policy. There are five stages of 'consequences' for unacceptable behaviour of which the last three involve 'time out' in class, 'time out' in another class and being sent to the 're-start room'. If behaviour is extreme a child may be sent to this room immediately. Its purpose is to provide a place for the child to continue their work and for a member of staff to talk to them about their behaviour; parents/carers are also informed at this stage. Although this excludes children temporarily from the teaching that is being experienced by their peers it is seen as a way of allowing the rest of the class to get on with their work without being disturbed. When introduced in 2000, approximately five to ten children a day were sent there. However, when we visited, a maximum of two to three children were sent each week and sometimes none at all.

In 2002 Ofsted drew attention to the school's low attendance figures (92.9 per cent) compared to national averages (93.9 per cent) and high unauthorised absences (3.2 per cent; national, 0.5 per cent). Since then the school has introduced new policies and practices and strengthened existing ones to help improve these figures. These include the 'attendance hotline' (phoning at least 50 per cent of parents on the first day of absence and 100 per cent by the second day); supporting parents who have difficulties getting their children to come to school; and rewarding children for full attendance.

Access to spaces and places

The school is not fully physically accessible because there is no lift in the two-storey building that houses the KS2 classrooms, although this was being rectified as part of the development programme. Because parts of the school are 50 years old, its physical appearance looks a little worn; however, much effort is put into making it colourful and welcoming. Each term the timetable is suspended for one afternoon a week, over a three week period, to allow children to undertake art work. This results in an array of high quality displays in shared areas such as the corridors and reception. Similarly, many classrooms are well-ordered and full of brightly coloured displays.

Staff emphasised the safe and welcoming nature of the school. Indeed, being 'safe' is built into the school's behaviour policy, where its relationship to successful learning is emphasised:

> It is every child's right to grow up and learn in an educational environment where they feel safe and happy and which will enable them to learn without being threatened, bullied, or badly treated.

Calm and ordered behaviour from the children and consistency in how that behaviour is managed by staff were presented as prerequisites for learning to take place. The headteacher described this as his main priority when joining the school. A teacher who came to Kingsley shortly before him remarked: 'When I first started we had some children climbing on the school roof and swearing … We don't see that extreme behaviour any more'.

Children's positive behaviour is reinforced through rewards in the form of praise, stickers and certificates, plus special events such as visits to the headteacher for the 'happy hour'. The term 'punishment' is not used, but rather 'consequences'. These are intended to provide children with the opportunity to reflect on their behaviour. There is a designated behaviour support teacher who has responsibility for helping children manage their behaviour. In all our observations we saw teachers offering firm but positive reinforcement of acceptable behaviour. Teachers rarely raised their voices and children were generally calm and polite. Individual incidents of concern were dealt with swiftly so as not to disturb the work of other children. We also observed the consistent application of the school's behaviour policies as they were put into practice by teachers.

There are clear induction policies and practices to welcome new members to the school: for staff, children and their families. For example, children who come to Kingsley outside the usual entry dates receive support from a learning mentor and, if appropriate, a teacher of English as an additional language. Teachers are expected to select a class buddy, talk to their class about being welcoming and find out about the child's recent history and experiences. Staff also work hard to make the school a welcoming place for parents/carers, who are encouraged to come into the classrooms at the beginning and end of each day to see their child's work and to talk to staff about any concerns they might have. Kingsley is also part of a local scheme, 'New Deals for Communities', which funds classes for adults, such as ICT, keep fit and family literacy.

Access to the curriculum

There is a structured timetable for all year groups, based around four sessions a day. It has two distinguishing features in which the influence of the national curriculum tests, taken in Years 2 and 6, is apparent. First, the balance between core (literacy, numeracy and science) and foundation (history, art, physical education, music and so forth) subjects changes over the course of the three terms for these year groups. As one teacher explained: '[After Christmas] our main focus is far more on getting results for SATs really. The foundation subjects are on the side to some extent'. Second, literacy and numeracy are 'blocked' across the timetable so that the 'setting' of children by attainment can take place in Years 2 to 6 (also science in Year 6 only). These sets are arranged so the groups for the 'highest' attaining children are larger than those for the 'lowest'. The three classes in each year are redistributed into three sets in Years 3, 4 and 5. However, in Years 2 and 6, a fourth teacher is provided: allowing the flexibility of even smaller sized groups or team teaching. For example, we observed the Year 6 'lowest' attainment literacy set in which nine children were present and also the 'highest' attainment numeracy set in which there were 23 children.

The headteacher argued that these arrangements were a strategic necessity because test results were so poor when he first came. 'Achievement is incremental … so if things in the rest of the school had been better we wouldn't have needed to push them in Years 2 and 6'. And, whilst he also described the tests as only one measure of a school's success, he argued strongly that the league tables are influential because of their impact on some parents when choosing a school, as well as on the recruitment and retention of staff. Thus if results started to fall he suggested that it could precipitate a downward spiral which would be damaging for the school generally.

In principle, all children participate in all curriculum areas. However, some are withdrawn from a number of timetabled lessons to work individually, or as part of a small group, mainly with staff from the learning support department. This is not to exclude them from mainstream activities but to provide additional and specialist support. Examples include the 'nurture' and the 'speech and language' groups for which the multi-sensory room in the department may be used. However, it is school policy that learning support staff chiefly work alongside children in class. As an LSA explained when discussing her work with a particular child: 'There is no point [her] being in the school if she's not with the others'.

As already noted, withdrawal from lessons also takes place when a child is sent to the 're-start room' because of unacceptable behaviour. In addition, small groups of children are withdrawn for 'behaviour support': a preventative programme intended to raise self-esteem and provide strategies for coping with difficult situations. Another form of withdrawal occurs as part of the school's 'gifted and talented' programme, involving about 30 children who are taken out of lessons for extension work, such as thinking skills.

Beyond the formal curriculum, Kingsley provides lunchtime and after school clubs and activities, including netball, cheerleading, basketball, football and dance. Outside trips and visits are also part of the school's wider curriculum. During one Year 4 lesson we noted discussions about a forthcoming trip to the Natural History Museum as well as to the cinema.

Participation and collaboration: learning together

Learning alongside other students

Kingsley, like most primary schools in England, arranges its children in mixed attainment classes according to age with, as far as possible, an equal distribution of boys and girls. However, as noted above, for the majority of children in Years 2 to 6, much of their learning occurs within sets rather than their class groups. So, for example, in the winter term of 2003, Year 6 children were taught in attainment sets for literacy, numeracy and science: or 14 out of 20 sessions each week. According to the headteacher, setting encourages 'frustrated children and the more able ... both [to be] pushed'. The Year 6 team leader also explained that it allows smaller group sizes for children with the 'lowest' attainment. Both maintained that these arrangements supported the academic achievement of all children and not just those at the extremes. Setting also takes place *within* classes, particularly for core curriculum subjects. For example, in the Year 6 'highest' attaining numeracy set, the children were split into five groups according to recent test results.

Of course, notions of achievement are relative, as indicated by the following comments made by an LSA talking about the progress of one child: 'They're small things but she'll take her own coat off and hang it up now and when she goes to the toilet she'll wash her own hands and pull up her pants. She didn't before'. This remark helps to illustrate the range of children's attainments and needs within the school. On the one hand, achievement is acknowledged in terms of a child hanging a coat on a peg and on the other, it is measured by a child gaining level four or five in their KS2 tests. This clearly makes great demands on teachers' skills in terms of presenting lessons which comprise learning tasks which are appropriate to all children. It is arguable that the school's policy on setting by attainment for many lessons helps to alleviate this. The use of setting by attainment *within* a class is another way that teachers address this concern.

Supporting students to learn together

Children learn not only from teachers and support staff but also from each other. Therefore it could be argued that the wider the range of children in a class, the greater the learning resources available. However, at Kingsley such opportunities are fairly limited; for example, we did not observe instances of older children working alongside younger ones. Also, the prevalence of setting reduces occasions when children who find learning less straightforward can be supported by their more able peers who, in turn, by taking on the role of 'teacher', are able to reinforce and extend their own understanding. Nevertheless, whatever the setting arrangements, every teaching group obviously comprises children with a range of knowledge, experiences, expertise and interests and we certainly observed many examples of children informally supporting one another in paired and group activities. For example, in a history lesson, in which the children were working in groups, the teacher made explicit not only what she wanted them to do but how she wanted them to work: 'collaboratively ... listening to one another ... sharing ideas ... helping one another ... these are important skills too'.

The role of LSAs and TAs (teaching assistants) in classrooms can also increase opportunities for children to learn together. However, the LSAs we observed mainly worked with individual children, thus limiting their scope to learn directly from their peers. The role of a TA was more flexible, although they were only allocated to classes in Years R, 1, 2 and 6. We observed TAs working with a range of children: making costumes for the school play, helping to produce cotton wool snowmen, listening to reading, working on spellings and so forth. They also responded skilfully to children's behaviour in ways which did not disrupt the teaching and learning of others.

Members of staff working together

There was clear evidence that teachers collaborated together in terms of planning schemes of work, sharing good practice and supporting one another when difficulties or concerns arose. Indeed, this was built into the school's staffing structure comprising the school leadership group, senior management team, curriculum co-ordinators and year group teams. The latter met every week to discuss teaching plans, with different members taking responsibility for particular areas. These plans were passed on to assistant headteachers who checked for content, quality and consistency. They were also given to support staff so they knew what would be happening in relevant classes. One teacher described her team as 'supportive, in all ways'. All teachers interviewed said they discussed their work and any associated concerns with a range of colleagues, including the headteacher. With regards to individual children's learning difficulties, they all said that they consulted the school's special educational needs co-ordinator (SENCO) and found doing so useful.

Teaching and support staff also seemed to work well together. Our observations provided evidence of the positive nature of these professional relationships. LSAs also described the support they received from the SENCO as being essential: 'When I get stuck or I don't know something, I ask her for help'. Similarly, when describing her role, the SENCO emphasised the importance of supporting the LSAs. She explained, they 'can feel isolated ... [it is] important [they] feel members of a team ... they might see five or six different teachers in the course of a day'.

Schools and other institutions working together

There appeared to be good links between teachers at Kingsley and their colleagues from the local secondary school, particularly with regards to preparing the transfer of Year 6 children. Staff also worked collaboratively with colleagues from the LA in a number of ways, including mentoring for newly qualified teachers, training courses for LSAs and specialist support from advisory teachers. The latter provided advice for staff on whole school issues, such as literacy, as well as guidance about supporting individual children with particular learning needs, such as those with sensory impairments. The training for LSAs seemed to be especially pertinent in terms of supporting the inclusion and achievement of a range of children. Staff also engaged in other forms of professional development: for example, some attended higher education courses or participated in training sessions at the school on topics such as British Sign Language and playground games.

Participation and diversity: recognition and acceptance

Recognition and acceptance of students, by staff

The school's prospectus states:

> We will aim to support every pupil to do their best in everything they do. We will develop and provide a caring, stimulating and secure environment. We will encourage a community spirit and actively promote mutual respect.

Whilst the stated aims of any school may be dismissed as tokenistic, there appeared to be amongst staff at Kingsley a genuine belief in valuing all children and their achievements. During our time in the school we overheard no derogatory comments from staff about any child. This is not to say that staff did not discuss difficulties they encountered when working with some children, but attitudes were respectful and considered. This was also reflected in the way in which staff managed children's behaviour with praise, good humour and encouragement.

There also appeared to be a strongly held belief that most, if not all, children can make progress and that all of them have the right to be supported to do their best. Whilst some teachers suggested that some family circumstances can have a detrimental effect on children's learning they also argued that Kingsley School can and does make a difference. 'We can't really change their home environment but we can accommodate for them in school, which is providing them with that opportunity'. Indeed, this optimism about making a positive difference to children's lives seemed to be a core belief shared amongst staff in the school.

This recognition and acceptance of children's worth was also demonstrated by the determination of staff to provide a safe, calm and caring environment to ensure that learning did take place and hence the emphasis on behaviour in the school. Indeed, it was children whose behaviour was particularly challenging who seemed the most demanding for staff to accept in terms of inclusion. Even so, the circumstances and needs of individual children appeared to be carefully considered. One teacher, when discussing the school's policy of contacting parents once a child has been sent to the 're-start room', also explained that this did not happen automatically. She gave the example of a boy who was on the Child Protection Register because of his violent mother, and who was frequently in trouble in lessons. This teacher thought his difficulties at school reflected his home experiences: asking his mother to come in to discuss his behaviour would not necessarily be in his best interests.

The attitudes of staff towards including the diversity of children who are designated as having special educational needs have already been discussed. As already noted, their main concerns were related to the lack of resources to support individual children rather than beliefs about their right to be present in the school. Comments by staff also suggested that initial reservations were generally tempered by subsequent experiences. One LSA explained:

> Initially I found it so daunting … But then when you start to get to know [the children] they are not so different … When they get upset they might shout a bit louder than another child but they are still saying, 'I'm upset' … If you're not working with them, or around them, then you wouldn't know.

Recognition and acceptance of staff, by staff

Many of the examples already provided indicate an accepting, tolerant and respectful attitude amongst staff towards each other. In the same way in which we heard no derogatory comments about children from staff, we also heard no negative remarks from staff about their colleagues. It seems likely that these corresponding findings are connected. That is, there is a belief shared amongst staff that not only can all children achieve, but also all staff have an important part to play in this endeavour. Our observations of the staffroom suggest that Kingsley is a friendly, lively and sociable workplace. There is a staff hierarchy in so far as staff are organised into a number of structures and groups. However, they provide numerous positions of responsibility so that the hierarchy is, in effect, relatively flat: allowing teachers opportunities to develop professionally. Indeed, some of these positions were created fairly recently with the intention of supporting the development and retention of key members of staff.

Finally, the role of the headteacher seems crucial in understanding Kingsley School. Those staff who remembered the school before his arrival remarked on the very positive influence he has had. Their respect for him as a colleague and their appreciation of the support he provides for them were conspicuous throughout. The following comment is typical: 'Staff were demoralised … not supported … especially when dealing with difficult children … That's changed now'. He explained that the 'most important and the most demanding' part of his job was to maintain the running of the school in such a way that his 'staff and children are happy to be here'.

Recognition and acceptance of students, by students

During our time at Kingsley we heard few negative comments and rarely observed any acts of unkindness amongst the children. Whilst it is clear from our interviews with staff that such instances did take place, it also seems likely that they did not happen frequently. In classrooms we saw children helping one another with spellings, sharpening pencils, reading 'difficult' words, sharing equipment and so forth. Such behaviour was particularly striking considering the high mobility of children in the school, including the way in which some arrive and depart at short notice, and the effects this probably has on all children in terms of building secure friendships.

We did not observe resentment about the extra support given to some children because of learning difficulties, nor hostility about teachers' allowances for differences in children's behaviour. For example, the actions of a child who tossed and turned during story time and sometimes groaned appeared to be accepted by her peers as part of who she is. The children's attitudes towards each other seem to have been nurtured within a culture of respect and tolerance, shaped by the attitudes they have experienced from and observed in the staff, and based on the core belief that all members of the school are valued.

Discussion

Kingsley Primary School has served its local community for some fifty years. During that time it has experienced substantial shifts in both the inclusion and achievement of its children. It is a school in which, because of challenging circumstances, staff might have been expected to show some resistance to the LA's inclusion policy and yet this case study illustrates their commitment to supporting the learning and participation of all children. In 2000, the LA was concerned that Kingsley might fail its next Ofsted inspection. Two years later when the inspectors visited, they described it as a 'good school' and, in the same year, it was selected by the DfES as one of the 'top one hundred most improved schools'. The stories behind this success highlight the determination of staff not only to improve the school's overall performance in national curriculum tests but also to maintain their principled approach to inclusion.

Measures of achievement: the impact of national curriculum tests

As already discussed in this book, national curriculum test results are often an inadequate measure by which to compare schools since they neither take account of the particular circumstances of an individual school, nor do they acknowledge alternative understandings of achievement. Nevertheless, these tests continue to influence the teaching and learning that takes place in many schools in England.

Certainly, Kingsley's headteacher was unequivocal about the pressures they exert on children and staff at his school: poor results were highly damaging, whilst improvements were likely to be beneficial. In particular, he argued, if Kingsley did not do well in the local league table its more middle-class families were likely to opt for other schools and this then upset the balance of its intake, pushing results down further. He also maintained that poor results had a detrimental effect on both the recruitment of new staff and the retention of existing ones. This in turn exerted additional pressures on those teachers who remained and lowered morale in the school generally. In contrast, when improvements took place in the school's Key Stage tests results, self-confidence amongst the staff was improved. Similarly, supporting children to achieve well in Key Stage 2 tests enhanced children's self-esteem as well as raised teachers' expectations about them when they reached secondary school.

It is in this context that the huge efforts to improve Key Stage results at Kingsley should be considered. Tables 5.1 and 5.2 provide figures for Key Stage 2 test results for the years 2000 to 2003. Over these four years Kingsley's results improved notably in mathematics and science, and the rate of improvement was faster than at both LA and national levels. Results for English also indicate some improvements although they appear to be less impressive; this discrepancy may well be a reflection of the high proportion of children who arrive at the school at an early stage of English language acquisition.

Whilst these tables record that improvements have been made in Key Stage 2 test results at Kingsley, they cannot show *how* this progress has been brought about. Particularly significant are changes to the curriculum in years two and six. These include: shifting the balance of the timetable towards the core curriculum and away from foundation subjects; providing extra staffing to support core subjects; and widespread setting and grouping of children by attainment. Whilst these developments have almost certainly contributed to the improvements in the school's test results, they may also have affected the children's achievement and inclusion in other ways.

Table 5.1 Key Stage 2 results 2000 and 2003

Children	English		Mathematics		Science	
achieving level 4 or above (%)	2000	2003	2000	2003	2000	2003
Kingsley	51%	65%	60%	87%	67%	99%
LA	64.8%	68.5%	64.1%	66.5%	78.7%	80.5%
England	75%	75%	72%	73%	85%	87%

Source: DfES website

Table 5.2 Improvement measure for Key Stage 2 SATs, 2000–3

Year	Kingsley	LA	England
2000	179	207.6	231
2001	204	215.5	233
2002	245	215.8	234
2003	250	215.5	234

Source: DfES website

First, there is a tension between improving test results and the provision of a broad and balanced curriculum. Timetabling arrangements, for children in years two and six, provided limited opportunities to meet their imaginative, creative and physical needs. This seems to be especially pertinent to those children whose lives are more troubled and/or those who would particularly benefit from learning through less academic means. Although efforts were made to counter this in the final half term of the year (after the tests), this may not compensate for the concentration on core subjects in the other five and a half terms.

Second, some staff were concerned about children's anxieties regarding the national curriculum tests including the nature of the sets and groups to which they had been assigned. Indeed, some children seemed very aware of the values ascribed to achieving different levels. Meanwhile, other staff argued that children were well supported *because* they were so thoroughly prepared for the tests. However, it is likely that the constant emphasis on the tests contributed to the difficulties experienced by some children.

Finally, it appears that the policy of setting for core subjects worked both for and against the achievement and the inclusion of some children in the school. It certainly allowed smaller sized 'lower attainment' groups which gave children who were less academically successful greater teacher contact. Also, by limiting the range of attainment in a group, the demands made of staff were reduced. However, it is not clear what the longer-term effects of these arrangements might have been on children's self-esteem as well as teachers' expectations about them. This seems particularly relevant to those children who were placed in 'lower' sets. Furthermore, the use of setting restricted opportunities for children to learn from, and support, others in their peer group: this too may have a detrimental effect on achievement. Finally, the decision to resource additional staffing in years two and six, partly to support the setting policy, had an indirect effect on resourcing decisions elsewhere in the school.

Measures of inclusion

Measuring inclusion is no less problematic than measuring achievement. According to figures provided in the introduction of this chapter, Kingsley had a relatively low number of children identified as having 'special educational needs' compared to both national and LA findings. However, inclusion is clearly about far more than such forms of categorisation. It seems clear that children at Kingsley had a range of needs, not necessarily represented in such figures, but which may be identified in other ways; for example, the large proportion of children eligible for free school meals as well as the school's high mobility rate (both above LA and national averages). Furthermore, very often conceptualisations of 'special educational needs' categories are context related and therefore necessarily open to interpretation. Some children at Kingsley who were not on the school's 'SEN register' may well have been if they had attended other schools.

More generally, the concept of inclusion seemed to be accepted as a core value within the school and amongst staff there appeared to be a strong determination to support the learning and participation of all children. Certainly, much good work was done by members of the learning support department, as well as by class teachers, to ensure its successful implementation in practice. However, at times, there was also some uncertainty about what provision might be best for those children with the greatest needs: in particular, whether to withdraw some children for specialist small group work or to provide in-class support.

Behaviour, achievement and inclusion

Staff at Kingsley were clear about the nature of the relationship between children's achievement and inclusion and teachers' management of their behaviour. Prior to the current headteacher's appointment, the disruptive and threatening actions of some children were of serious concern to staff, parents and other children. Creating the calm and safe atmosphere which now prevails in the school has allowed far greater opportunities for successful teaching and learning to take place and, as such, has undoubtedly contributed to higher levels of achievement and inclusion.

Nonetheless, this strong emphasis on managing behaviour seems to have encouraged some teachers, sometimes, to focus on safe approaches to teaching, rather than take risks with more creative ones. In this way, the potential for a few children to misbehave may have affected the learning of others. On the one hand, classroom order must, of course, be maintained; on the other hand, it seems important to be able to challenge and excite children about their learning. Now that the behaviour policies and practices have been so well established in the school, it may be that a wider range of teaching and learning approaches could be introduced.

Concluding remarks

It seems that staff at Kingsley share core values about the purpose of education and their role as educators, and these have been crucial in supporting both the achievement and the inclusion of children at the school. Underpinning their work is the belief that all children are of equal worth, regardless of gender, ethnicity, language, home circumstances and/or particular learning needs. These values and beliefs are embedded in the policies and practices of the school, as well as in the countless everyday interactions that take place amongst its members. Meanwhile, the complex and demanding nature of their work is illustrated by the careful balancing act in which they are engaged. That is, whilst being attentive to the school's performance in national curriculum tests, they continue to be vigilant about managing classroom behaviour and, at the same time, maintain their principled approach to supporting the learning and participation of all children in their care.

6   Amadeus Primary School

Introducing Amadeus Primary School

Amadeus is a new co-educational community school for pupils aged 3 to 11. It provides places for children living on a recently built and rapidly expanding housing estate. The school officially opened in January 2000, with a pupil intake of 116, which had risen to 368 when we first visited the school in 2003. By 2005 the total number on the roll was 411, and it seems likely that these figures will become more steady now a full cohort of children has gone through the school from reception to Year 6. In its first few years, the school experienced a high degree of mobility amongst its pupil population, although this too is likely to become more settled once numbers stabilise. In its first Ofsted report in 2001 the inspectors described Amadeus as 'a good school, which, in a short time, has established itself at the heart of this new community'.

The school itself is strikingly attractive both inside and out, with light and airy rooms and spaces to play. It is also well resourced: for example, there is a purpose-built IT and library suite and each classroom has its own separate quiet and messy areas. The site has been designed to be fully accessible to all members of the community: it is built on one level with wide corridors and doors, and has good hygiene facilities, low dado rails to support children with visual impairments and a hearing induction loop system.

The school serves a culturally diverse, but economically depressed area. The majority of the children live on the local housing estate, and very few families own their homes. The 2001 Ofsted report noted that over 70 per cent of pupils were entitled to free school meals, which was well above the then national average of 18 per cent and considerably more than the LA average of 40 per cent. The local community comprises families from a range of different ethnic backgrounds. The 2001 Ofsted report also noted that over 57 per cent of the children spoke English as an additional language and that there were 18 different languages spoken in the school. In 2001, approximately 32 per cent of the children were on the school's register of special educational needs. By 2003, when we visited the school, the numbers had fallen to about 27 per cent. Staffing at the school reflects the growing pupil population. In 2000, Ofsted recorded 11 (full-time equivalent) teachers for reception to Year 6, plus an additional two teachers for the nursery. They also noted there were a further 11 education support staff. In 2003 this had grown to over 40 staff in total, plus four music instructors.

Examining inclusion and achievement

In this section we present our findings from the case study of Amadeus School, using the main headings of the *Framework for Participation.*

Participation and access: being there

Joining the school

The formal admissions policy for Amadeus is in line with other community schools in the LA; that is, all children who live locally are welcome to attend this fully inclusive school. There is no barrier to the admission of children with physical disabilities because of the high level of facilities, specialised equipment and staff expertise in the school. The school has a natural catchment area formed primarily by the housing estate in which it is located.

Since the school opened in 2000, the numbers of children on the roll have increased each year, not only as new children have joined the nursery and reception classes and then grown up through the school, but also when older children arrive at Amadeus having previously attended a different school. Some are new to the area and their presence at the school is a reflection of the mobile local population. However, others, albeit in small numbers, have come to Amadeus following a permanent exclusion from nearby schools, usually because of behaviour deemed to be unacceptable. The headteacher argued that the LA expected her to admit excluded children to her school because of surplus places. This was particularly applicable when the school was new and still growing to full capacity.

In interviews, staff maintained that Amadeus was able to meet the needs of all its children. They also argued that including children with a range of identified learning difficulties did not have a negative effect on the school more generally. One member of staff, who was also the parent of two children at the school, stated: 'Do I think my children are deprived because there is a child with special educational needs in the classroom? No, in a word'. However, there was a general concern amongst staff about including those children whose behaviour was considered to be challenging, particularly when they had already been excluded from another school. Two main reasons were given. First, that some children would never cope with mainstream provision: 'They do merge in. [But] there are some characters who will never merge whatever school they go to'. Second, that it was necessary to maintain a balance across the school and within individual classrooms, and that being 'forced' by the LA to accept too many children with challenging behaviour had a negative effect on the rest of the school. In such instances some staff argued that a specialised placement might be more appropriate, perhaps part time.

Staying in the school

The school's 2001 Ofsted report records that in that school year no permanent exclusions and three fixed term exclusions took place. However, different forms of temporary internal exclusions are used to address particular behaviour problems. For example, if a child misbehaves repeatedly during lunchtimes s/he will be sent home for lunch. One Teaching Assistant (TA) described this practice as being an 'inconvenience for parents', and therefore an effective way of gaining their involvement in supporting the school to address their child's behavioural concerns.

Attendance at the school was noted in the 2001 Ofsted report as being a matter of concern, with figures for both authorised (6.1 per cent) and unauthorised (0.9 per cent) absences above the national average for that year (5.4 per cent and 0.5 per cent respectively). When we visited in 2003, new policies and practices had been put into place for recording and monitoring absence. By 2005, attendance figures had shown some improvement (authorised absences, 5.1 per cent; unauthorised, 0.8 per cent).

Access to spaces and places

As noted in the introduction to this chapter, Amadeus is not only fully accessible to children and adults with physical disabilities, the site has also been designed so as to encourage children with disabilities to develop independence and confidence. The school buildings and grounds are attractive and welcoming to all children, their families, staff and visitors. There are places to sit and be quiet and also spaces to be play games and be noisy. All the classrooms open onto play areas enabling easy access to outdoor activities without concerns about overcrowding in enclosed cloakrooms or corridors. The reception area is brightly decorated with children's art work and there are a number of other attractive large-scale displays throughout the communal areas and within individual classrooms. When new children join the school they are assigned a peer mentor or 'buddy'. This system is also used to support some current children, particularly those who may be vulnerable to bullying and/or being isolated during lunch or play times.

Maintaining safe and orderly classrooms is also a high priority for the school. The headteacher and class teachers described their concerns about a few children whose behaviours could potentially significantly disrupt the learning of others. They also noted that the families of some children were extremely difficult and complex, describing lives disrupted by poverty, drugs, violence or neglect. They recognised that children inevitably brought aspects of their home circumstances into school and these shaped their behaviour.

To support both staff and children, the school has in place a clear behaviour policy based on the 'traffic lights' system for recording and monitoring behaviour. There was a traffic lights chart on display in every classroom we visited and in all the lessons we observed we saw evidence of this policy being made use of in practice. The aim is for children to stay on 'green' but following a misdemeanour they may be moved to 'amber'. If another incident takes place that day they may go to 'red', which would then require a visit to the headteacher. However, it is also possible for a child to move back to 'green' if they demonstrate 'good' behaviour, perhaps by working diligently or an act of kindness towards a peer. Furthermore, as one member of staff explained, 'Every child starts the day on green … [because] every day is a new day'. We also noted how responsive many of the children were to the range of rewards available in the school. Some, such as stickers and certificates, are for individual children. Others are for whole classes, such as 'golden time' usually announced on Friday afternoon assemblies, and providing prizes such as extra playtime or a sweet for everyone in the class.

Access to the curriculum

> We believe that everyone is capable of participating successfully in the arts. An arts-based curriculum engages the children's interest, encourages creativity, thinking skills, cooperative working and positive behaviour. It addresses the different learning styles that children possess and makes the curriculum particularly accessible to our large number of children who speak English as an additional language. The arts provide a level playing field where all can contribute and many will excel.
>
> (Headteacher)

Like the majority of maintained primary schools in England, staff at Amadeus are expected to take into account the broad expectations of the national curriculum in terms of the content of what they teach. However, unlike many other schools, there is a most distinctive cross-curricular emphasis on teaching and learning through the performing arts. This approach has been established by the headteacher who is highly committed, indeed passionate, about all children having access to the curriculum through music, dance, drama, philosophy, painting, drawing and sculpture. These are presented not only as worthwhile activities in their own right but more importantly as the means by which teaching and learning can take place. It is the arts, therefore, which shape the school's overall curriculum rather than the national curriculum per se. This is reflected in interviews with staff across the school, in which very few references were made to Key Stage levels of attainment or league tables, but in which music, drama, art and so forth were constant themes.

This is supported by our observations. So, in one class, children extended their understanding of mathematical symmetry through dance; in another class the concept of adverbs was introduced through mime and role play; in another, a philosophy lesson began with a debate around the question 'What if time stopped?'; in an assembly, each class performed a different song to the rest of the school. Furthermore, in a number of lessons background music was played: for example, during one afternoon we heard Vivaldi, followed by Mozart and later some Bach. Whole school arts programmes include artists-in-residence, and violin or cello instruction for all children at Key Stage 1, as well as frequent opportunities to perform publicly in dance, music and drama.

All children are expected to participate in, and to benefit from, these activities regardless of their attainment levels or whether or not they are perceived as experiencing learning difficulties. Indeed, teaching staff repeatedly stressed the importance of the arts in making the curriculum accessible to a greater range of children. Furthermore, some teachers also argued their own teaching was improved through this focus. As one member of staff explained: 'Teaching creatively ... is what we do well ... we teach through drama, dance, art, and music ... [it] lets us express ourselves as teachers'.

Because of this emphasis on the arts, the headteacher also supports a cross-curricular project approach to learning rather than separate timetabled lessons for discrete subjects. As one teacher noted, staff are encouraged to be flexible about timetabling: 'We will carry on teaching if we feel like our objectives haven't been met and the children are engaged and motivated and enjoying the subject'. In all interviews with staff we heard similar expressions of support for this non-traditional approach to the timetable and we certainly observed a number of lessons that demonstrated this commitment. However, other lessons we saw were perhaps more conventional. That is, the teaching was based around subject areas such as literacy, numeracy, science, physical education and so forth. Some lessons were also conventional in their structure: often starting with whole class demonstrations and discussions and then children working individually whilst seated in small groups.

Within these broad parameters, and however the lessons are organised and whatever their content, some modification of teaching takes place to support the learning of individual children who have been identified as having special educational needs. This work is managed by the special educational needs co-ordinator who is assisted by the School Mentor. The responsibilities of the latter include meeting with certain children on a weekly basis to monitor their requirements for learning support. In addition, any child can ask to see her about a range of issues, 'anything from being disaffected to being bullied ... attendance'.

In terms of access to the wider curriculum, Amadeus School offers a broad range of activities within the school and as outside trips and visits. Many of these are related to the emphasis on the arts. All children are expected to be involved in school performances and extra music lessons are provided at lunchtimes. Visits include opportunities to see professional productions as well as to be involved in working alongside professional artists. For example, there was a recent trip to play alongside a professional orchestra.

Participation and collaboration: learning together

Learning alongside other students

Typically for English primary schools, children at Amadeus are mainly taught in classes organised according to age (by year group), gender (a balance as far as possible of girls and boys) and attainment (mixed). Almost all teaching and learning takes place within these arrangements, although there is some withdrawal of individual and small groups of children for additional support in basic skills. Furthermore, opportunities are also provided for older children to work with younger ones. For example, on 'World Book Day' mixed age groups of children worked together; school productions also offer similar experiences.

Within the classes themselves we observed the use of a range of different organisational structures, including whole class, small group, paired and individual work. When in groups, children were most typically arranged by mixed attainment and gender for most curriculum subjects. However, for literacy and numeracy they were more likely to be grouped according to the teacher's assessment of their ability, usually at three or four levels. When teachers were interviewed about these groups they described them in general terms of '[he] needs some support' or '[she] is working really well at the moment'. None referred to the groups in terms of children's expected levels of attainment on national curriculum tests.

More broadly, the teachers we interviewed argued that a strength of the arts-based curriculum is that it provides opportunities for all children to learn together because of the nature of the learning tasks involved. For example, one teacher noted that philosophy lessons are accessible 'Because they [children] can all listen and they can all speak. So they start at the same level, and there is a real sense of equality'. Another teacher described a science lesson which focused on the habitats of different animals. She chose to teach this through the medium of dance.

> You are going to have your different learners: your visual learners, your physical learners ... So rather than the children sitting and learning about habitats, we'll get up. We did a whole dance based on habitats, to explore different habitats, and how different animals adapted to their situations. We met all our science objectives, but we were teaching through dance.

Supporting students to learn together

Teachers at Amadeus generally made good use of the grouping arrangements for children within their classes so as to encourage them to use each other as resources for learning. Sometimes particular collaborative strategies were put in place by the teacher. For example, in a philosophy lesson we observed, children were asked to work in pairs so as to develop and challenge each other's ideas; in a literacy lesson children were also paired so that a 'good' speller could support their partner's work. More commonly, however, we observed members of groups collaborating in a more *ad hoc*, but nevertheless worthwhile, manner: sharing equipment, praising one another's efforts, offering suggestions for spellings and multiplication tables, and so forth. Teachers generally encouraged and reinforced these sorts of behaviours through verbal reminders and praise.

Each class is allocated a designated TA to work alongside the teacher to support the learning of children identified as having special educational needs.

All teachers interviewed noted that they found this provision to be effective. In our observations we noted that the vast majority of the time that TAs were in lessons was spent working alongside individual and groups of children in ways that promoted their collaborative learning with other children. Even though, in some instances, a TA was allocated to one particular named child, they seemed careful about achieving a balance between focusing on that child and allowing them to develop more independent learning, whilst also offering broader support to the class as a whole. As one TA explained:

> [Child's name] will often say, 'I don't need you today, thank you'. So I tend to sit with the whole table, not always next to [him] … Maybe on a diagonal so that I can watch him, but be available for the other children … letting him see that I am not just being on his shoulder. That he enjoys. He enjoys his independence.

Perhaps more unusual is that some staff have the opportunity to experience participating in learning alongside children in the school. That is, violin and cello lessons are offered to teachers as well. This provides children with the experience of seeing their teachers genuinely learning with them: making mistakes, being frustrated and becoming more skilful. As one teacher explained: 'We all have the sense of being learners together. I [didn't] play an instrument … [we] are learning together … and we are all at the same stage'.

Members of staff working together

In all our interviews, staff (teaching and non-teaching) expressed a strong sense of working together as a team on behalf of the children in the school. This is partly derived from the headteacher's insistence that everyone has a 'shared vision' about the value of teaching and learning through an arts-based curriculum. And, at the same time, staff who hold this conviction are very likely to have common interests in music, drama, dance and art which also strengthen their sense of collegiality. Furthermore, even relatively inexperienced teachers are given opportunities to take some cross-school responsibilities (for example, subject co-ordination, such as literacy or music) which encourages collaborative working practices.

Teaching and support staff appear to work well together. As one teacher noted:

> There is not a great divide between support staff and teachers … the TAs will often take the class and take story time. And, they work with groups and things like that … I think we are really lucky we've got such brilliant TAs.

Support staff also explained how their experience and knowledge of particular children are valued and used by teachers. One described her work with a child who had been causing some concern and the short-term and longer-term strategies that were put into place to support his inclusion and achievement.

[He was] being sent out of class, wasn't settled, and things like that. So I went in there for an hour a day and, over a period of time, we noticed that it was just around literacy ... The class teacher and I met again and ... [I] said, 'OK, let me come in for literacy, then, let's not have him come out' ... And the progression [has been] amazing ... It was the observations, the class teacher talking to me, me talking to her, a bit of input from a literacy adviser who was on hand ... Now I'm working on [his] feelings and different issues that he has and things like that, because he has gone through that barrier with the writing.

Schools and other institutions working together

Staff at Amadeus work with a variety of colleagues outside the school. They make some use of the LA's specialist teachers who are able to offer teachers and TAs professional support for children identified as having special educational needs. They also draw on the LA for advice on particular curriculum areas, such as literacy. The headteacher also draws on other organisations if she considers them able to provide more effective services, in terms of both quality and cost. For example, the school has hired its own speech and language therapists and physiotherapists to work with staff and children. The headteacher has also paid for business management consultants from the private sector to help her produce a school management/business plan.

Amadeus is also part of a Networked Learning Community (a national scheme set up by the DfES via the National College of School Leadership). This comprises a number of local primary schools and their main feeder secondary school. The focus of this particular network has been to develop an arts curriculum across the schools. The headteacher explained that she is concerned that when children from Amadeus go on to secondary education they are far advanced in terms of their arts learning compared to children from other primary schools. Her intention then is to encourage other primary schools to 'catch up' with those from Amadeus and also to encourage colleagues from the secondary school to be more involved. Amadeus has also developed links with the arts community generally and particularly with those from music; for example, a professional orchestra was working with children over the period of our visits. Much of the funding for the music programme at the school is underwritten by local private business sponsors.

Participation and diversity: recognition and acceptance

Recognition and acceptance of children, by staff

From our interviews and observations, staff appear to act with respect and care towards children at Amadeus School. This is not to argue that all behaviours of children are considered acceptable, but rather that the prevailing attitude of adults in the school seems to be supportive and understanding. One member of staff explained:

> If you've got some children with problems at home, they are not like the average child that can come into school, sit in a whole classroom ... They might be thinking about what is happening at home. So that does affect their learning.

This willingness to take account of family and home circumstances was reiterated by a number of staff. At the same time they also expressed an optimism and determination that they should not be seen as an excuse for low expectations about children's achievements.

Children are also treated with respect in other ways. For example, they are encouraged to make choices about their learning and their opinions are listened to and seem to be valued. In the lessons we observed children were given opportunities to discuss their ideas and feelings in whole class and group discussions. The philosophy lessons were an example of this, but there were many others. One teacher liked to ask her class what they would like to learn and when: 'Should we do maths first or English first ... What do you feel like doing this morning? I can do either. So, how are you feeling, what do you want to do? Maybe we'll leave maths till this afternoon'. Another teacher invites her class to debate and then choose their 'rule of the week'.

Children who have been identified as having learning difficulties and/or disabilities seem to be fully accepted and included in school life. That is, their particular needs are taken into account as are the needs of any of the children. So, in a physical education lesson the 'rules' of a ball game were adapted to ensure that a child with a physical disability participated with his peers. This willingness to accommodate diversity is seen in other ways across the school; for example, teachers' planning of homework to fit the demands made on those children who study at the local mosque after school. An everyday example of responding sensitively to children's needs was provided by a TA:

> For children that are late being picked up, you can always offer them ... a glass of milk, squash or a piece of fruit ... like you would your own child who just arrived home from school ... it is not their fault that their parents are late or stuck in traffic.

Finally, the arts-based curriculum also appears to be an important means of respecting and including all children. In interviews, staff argued that it allows children access to a wider world from which they would otherwise probably be excluded both socially and economically. One member of staff explained:

> I think it opens you up, instead of being a stereotypical, you know, from [names local area], you've been exposed to, the other side of life as well ... I have two grandsons, both born [locally] ... I just think if the children can grasp this opportunity, to see things that are different.

There is no straightforward evidence to offer for this, however there is an intangible sense that offering the arts to the children is indicative of their worth as people.

Recognition and acceptance of staff, by staff

As already noted throughout this chapter, staff at Amadeus School seem to work well together. Both teachers and support staff spoke respectfully about their colleagues and appeared to value the contributions that different members could make to teaching and learning in the school. These attitudes seem to be underpinned by a shared belief that they are working in a school which is somehow 'special'. The focus on the arts and the nature of the school's catchment area provide staff with a collective sense of being involved in an unusual and demanding but highly rewarding enterprise. A TA explained that using the arts as a medium for learning also allows 'The school ... to change things, to brighten the day, to make the day different. Yes, we [have] to do our numeracy and ... our literacy but we can do it in different ways'.

This sense of being 'special' and 'different' is reflected in the way staff spoke about how lucky they thought they were to teach at Amadeus. One teacher asserted: 'It's been a fantastic experience for me, it really has ... I can't imagine going to ... another school like this where you are given the freedom to be the teacher that you want to be'. Another stated: 'I do enjoy teaching here. Yes, I love it. I can't see myself going anywhere, not for a while'. This sense of good fortune seems to permeate their commitment not only towards the children, as noted previously, but also to one another.

The role of the headteacher also appears to be crucial here. Staff talked about how she encourages them to be experimental in their teaching. One teacher described how, when she first joined the school, she was struggling to keep to the prescribed timings for different parts of the literacy hour:

> [The headteacher] said to me one day, look, this is not how we do things here, if it takes longer then that's how we will do it ... That's very much the philosophy of Amadeus. We're really encouraged to be ourselves and not put on some kind of teacher act. Just to be ourselves with the children. We're all encouraged to say, well I don't know the answer or, no, I made a mistake there ... and teaching creatively as well.

In these ways the headteacher helps to create a culture in which teachers expect their work to involve being highly creative, motivating and responsive to children's changing needs.

Recognition and acceptance of children, by children

The general behaviour and attitudes of children towards one another appeared to model those that were shown to them by staff and that they observed during interactions between staff. In lessons, assemblies and playtimes we noted that the vast majority of children conducted themselves in a friendly, helpful and kind manner. This is not to suggest that no child ever acts unkindly towards another or that bullying does not take place sometimes at Amadeus. However, we did not observe any such incidents. Furthermore, a member of staff, who is also the parent of children in the school, argued that including children with disabilities and/or learning difficulties is a positive experience for all in the school: 'For children, like my children, to work with children and help them and have the knowledge of that. As a society it is quite important ... I saw my daughter interacting yesterday ... She automatically went up and helped [another child]'.

Discussion

In some ways Amadeus is similar to the vast majority of primary schools in England: children attend from the local community; they are arranged in classes based on year groups of mixed boys and girls; what they are taught broadly fulfils the demands of the national curriculum; and their achievements are partly assessed through national tests at Key Stages 1 and 2. In addition, the school shares a number of characteristics with other primary schools in the same local authority: it adheres to the LA's policy of full inclusion; it serves a culturally diverse but economically depressed urban area; teaching and support staff seem determined to support the learning and participation of all its children.

Achievement and inclusion through the arts

In other ways, however, Amadeus may be considered to be rather unusual in that its arts-focused, project-based curriculum is atypical of many schools both locally and nationally. Whilst most primary schools in England also teach some music, dance, drama and so forth, at Amadeus the arts are integral to the entire curriculum. As noted throughout the previous sections, staff at the school are able to present a cogent argument that this approach supports both the inclusion and the achievement of all children. Indeed, it is also possible to argue that it supports the inclusion and achievement of staff. The following offers a summary of related key issues raised.

At Amadeus School the arts-based curriculum provides:

- a medium through which all learning can take place; it is not about teaching the arts, per se, although they too are valuable in their own right.
- opportunities for all children to gain access to the curriculum regardless of their prior attainments, difficulties in learning, disabilities and any other changing needs.
- learning experiences for children, and teaching experiences for staff, which are creative, motivating and exciting.
- opportunities for children to experience successful learning in a variety of different ways: visually, aurally, actively, intellectually, etc.
- a coherent set of beliefs shared by children and staff, including a sense of the school being 'special' and its members being valued.
- a means by which children and staff are able to assess their achievements, in terms of progress and performance, in a wide range of different ways rather than focusing primarily on Key Stage national assessment levels.

The points above may seem to present a rather rosy view of the school. As noted earlier, some lessons we observed were actually fairly conventional in their structure, content and presentation. Also, managing the classroom behaviour of a few children seemed to be of real concern for some staff, who argued that a small number had the potential to disrupt the learning of many others. Furthermore, the family lives of some children were particularly difficult and complex and this too had an impact on their experiences at school. Nevertheless, the culture of Amadeus seems to be shaped by its arts-based curriculum which is premised on valuing all children and believing that each one can achieve in his/her own way. The role of the headteacher in leading and maintaining this core philosophy should not be underestimated.

Ignoring the tests, achieving progress

Because of her conviction about the place of the arts in teaching and learning, the headteacher explained she was unwilling to shape the school's curriculum and timetable so as to 'prepare' children for Key Stage national tests. That is, she does not want staff to alter their teaching during the spring and summer terms to coach children for the tests in English, mathematics and science. Nor does she expect teachers to organise their classes to target children who are, say, borderline levels three/four or four/five at Key Stage 2. Both of these strategies are, however, common practice in many English primary schools. This is not to suggest that the headteacher was uninterested in the school's performance in the national assessment tests, but she maintained that an arts approach to the curriculum is a more effective way of supporting children's learning which, in the long term, would be reflected in the school's test results.

Of course, and as discussed earlier in the book, determining the achievement of an individual child is not straightforward. Trying to make sense of this across a whole school is even more complex. Whilst the national tests at Key Stages 1 and 2 are one form of measurement, they are clearly problematic. For Amadeus they are particularly difficult to use in terms of assessing progress over time because the school is still so new. There are no Key Stage 2 test results for the school until 2001. In our other case studies we have predominantly relied on information that was available before and during the school year in which we visited. For Amadeus, however, we have chosen to consider more recent results. Even then, making comparisons between this school's results and others in the LA, and/or nationally, is complicated, not least because it was not until 2006 that the first cohort of children who joined in reception took their Key Stage 2 national tests. Until then all results had been based on children who had attended at least one other school. Additionally, in some year groups, there are a disproportionate number of troubled and troubling children who have been permanently excluded from other schools. It is within this context that Tables 6.1–6.5 should be considered.

If national assessment tests are to be used as a measurement of achievement, then it seems that children at Amadeus School have made steady progress in all three subjects areas. This is most notable in mathematics and science, in which,

Table 6.1   KS2 English test results, 2001–5

Children achieving level 4 or above, English	2001	2002	2003	2004	2005
Amadeus	48%	79%	47%	79%	76%
Local authority	66.7%	64.5%	68.5%	71%	72%
England	75%	75%	75%	78%	79%

Source: DfES website

Table 6.2   KS2 Mathematics test results, 2001–5

Children achieving level 4 or above, Mathematics	2001	2002	2003	2004	2005
Amadeus	66%	59%	33%	74%	92%
Local authority	65.5%	69.2%	66.5%	70%	72%
England	71%	73%	73%	74%	75%

Source: DfES website

Table 6.3   KS2 Science test results, 2001–5

Children achieving level 4 or above, in Science	2001	2002	2003	2004	2005
Amadeus	86%	76%	60%	86%	97%
Local authority	83.3%	82%	80.5%	82%	84%
England	87%	86%	87%	86%	86%

Source: DfES website

Table 6.4   Improvement measure for KS2 test, 2001–5

Year	Amadeus	LEA	England
2001	200	215.5	233
2002	214	215.8	234
2003	140	215.5	234
2004	240	223	237
2005	266	231	240

Source: DfES website

Table 6.5   Children in Year 6 at Amadeus Primary School

Number of children	2001	2002	2003	2004	2005
Total	29	29	30	43	38
Identified as having special educational needs	12 (41.4%)	12 (41.4%)	23 (76.6%)	19 (44.2%)	19 (50%)

Source: DfES website

for 2005, the scores were far higher than national averages. However, there is a conspicuous anomaly in the school's results for 2003, about which Table 6.5 can perhaps provide some insight. In that particular year group over 76 per cent of the children taking the KS2 tests were identified as having special educational needs. Whilst the proportion at Amadeus, across every year from 2001 to 2005, is above the national average, this figure is especially high, and it seems likely that it will have skewed the results. It may be related to the school's acceptance, when it first opened, of children who had been excluded elsewhere, which created an imbalance amongst that cohort. More importantly, what none of these tables is able to identify are the wider achievements of all the children who have participated in the school's arts-based curriculum; nor can the tables predict what lasting effects this experience may have on them in terms of their achievement and inclusion in education more generally.

We would like to thank Stephen Jull for his contribution to the collection of evidence for this case study.

7   Harbour Community School

Brief profile of the school

Harbour Community School is a co-educational comprehensive school for students aged 11 to 16. It admits eight forms of entry, there are 240 students in each year group and the school has about 1,200 students on the roll. The catchment area of the school is predominantly white working class and there are high levels of poverty with many of the students living in economically difficult circumstances. The school reports significant social and health problems in the neighbourhood including TB, HIV infection and drug addiction. Most students come from the local community except for the 'resourced provision' for students designated as having profound and multiple learning difficulties, which serves the whole LA. Table 7.1 provides some demographic details of the school and LA population for one recent cohort of Year 11 pupils.

The school is located in modern buildings that opened in 1999 near redeveloped docklands. The building is accessible, although space is tight for the number of

Table 7.1   Percentages of Year 11 students on selected variables in Harbour School and the LA, 2004

School	Harbour School (n=212)	LA (n=3,267)
Total % SEN	**42.4**	18.5
Gender	53.3 boys	47.8 boys
	45.8 girls	48.1 girls
% FSM eligibility	**26.4**	39.6
First language other than English	**24.5**	57.3
Ethnicity (above 5%)	**65.6 White British**	19.4 White British
	11.8 Black African	15.5 Indian
		12.2 Pakistani
		11.8 Bangladeshi
		9.1 Black African
		7.7 Black Caribbean
Stability (% students in school since Year 7)	84.4	79.9

NB: Figures in bold are statistically significant when compared to all schools in the authority. Not all percentages add to 100 because of missing data.

students and some of the rooms used for teaching students identified as having special needs are too small. It has its own playing fields and a sports hall.

Evidence of inclusion and links to achievement

Participation and access: being there

The headteacher has been in post since 1999 when the new school opened. She has a strong background in post-19 education and experience in meeting the needs of a diverse range of students. She has a clear and pragmatic view of inclusion. At first, the head saw inclusion as being concerned with having children with special needs in the school, in other words it was about location. Subsequently the school began to work on the social and pedagogical aspects of inclusion. In addition, the definition of inclusion was broadened so that it was not just about children designated as having special needs or disability but also considered issues of race, gender and social class. The head stated that, 'in this school we talk about respect for human beings. Inclusion means all people are worthy of respect and are valued'.

Joining the school

There are five main feeder primary schools with the majority of the student intake being very local. In addition the school provides an authority-wide facility for about six students in each year group who are described as having profound and multiple learning difficulties. Additional resources are provided for these students and also for many others identified as having special educational needs, about one-third of the school population. Currently there are about fifty-five students (5 per cent) with a statement of special educational needs (it was 100 until a few years ago but changes in local authority policy have led to a decrease in numbers). Across the whole school a further 27.5 per cent of students are designated as having special needs but do not have a statement. The school employs a large team of special education staff (teachers and assistants) who work in targeted ways with identified students.

More than a quarter of students are reported as being eligible for free school meals but it is claimed that the true figure is nearer 80 per cent. Ofsted reports that the percentage of students speaking English as an additional language (25 per cent) is significantly higher than the national average; however, this figure is lower than the local authority average and the school has a higher proportion of native English speaking students than the local authority average (see Table 7.1). It is estimated that children speak around fifty different languages at home.

The headteacher says that the variable quality of the information about individual students arriving from feeder primary schools means that the school is often ill prepared for meeting the needs of some students. Although students with statements of special educational needs and those who are recipients of the resourced provision have clearly identified needs, some parents are recommended to place their child at the school but their needs only become evident later. In response to this lack of information about students, a Year 7 project was established to help with the transition of students from primary to the secondary school. Two members of the project team and learning mentors have been involved in preparing students for transfer and getting information about students from the primary schools. This is seen as a much more helpful way to manage the transition process.

The school employs 86 teachers, and there are 140 staff in total. Like many schools in this part of London, recruitment and retention of teachers is difficult. A significant proportion of the teaching staff are recruited from overseas and they have to be inducted into teaching in such a school.

The senior management of the school consists of a headteacher, a deputy head and an acting deputy. One of the two assistant heads is the special needs co-ordinator (SENCO). Previously he was deputy head of a large special school for 14 years. In addition there are three 'special needs' teachers, who have other management functions in the school, as well as other members of the learning support department. The assistant SENCO for Key Stage 3 (KS3) has been in post for four years. Previously he was part of the authority's learning support service. He has a diploma in dyslexia and is currently working on a KS3 curriculum project for students identified as having special educational needs and is in charge of Year 8 and Year 9 learning support. There is also a large team of learning support assistants.

Staying in the school and moving on

Levels of mobility in the school are high, reflecting the transient nature of the local community, with as many as 30 students arriving and leaving each term. Mobility makes it difficult to monitor achievement and plan provision. However, recent figures suggest that mobility is about the same as the local authority average.

The most recent Ofsted report indicates that the permanent exclusion of students was low for a school of this nature but temporary exclusions were high. More recently, permanent exclusions have risen. However, fewer students are now leaving the school in Years 10 and 11 to go to alternative provision (known as 'education otherwise') because the school now has to pay for such placements and there are now more suitable options available in the school.

There is real concern amongst staff about post-16 provision for students identified as having special needs when they leave the school. Links do exist for post-school transition but there are few resources to support this process. This is a particular problem for students who have severe learning difficulties; in part this is because once they have left school they no longer have statements to protect their needs, and future provision depends on goodwill and the willingness of providers to cooperate. Some colleges of further education seem unwilling to accept them as students. Because staff turnover is high in this area, particular challenges are raised for the development of staff expertise and consistency of approach.

Access to spaces and places

The school is relatively modern and has a light and airy feel. However, there are difficulties with aspects of the building, including acoustics and accessibility. The resourced provision base consists of two classrooms for the 35 to 40 students described as having profound and multiple learning difficulties and/or severe learning difficulties. The rooms are rather small and do not accommodate wheelchairs comfortably, making it difficult for students or staff to move around the rooms. The base is located in the centre of the school, at the end of the English corridor. In addition to the students mentioned above, the resourced provision also includes students who are seen as having moderate learning difficulties or physical impairments. Within this broader group, three students are described as having autism and a range of associated learning and communication difficulties and one student has multisensory impairment.

According to the SENCO, all resourced provision students attend some mainstream classes on an *ad hoc* basis according to their capacity. Students are not in the mainstream class all the time but for the most part are working within the national curriculum. They are taught in one of the two resourced provision rooms for up to 20 hours a week, but all go out for at least one lesson per day. The main aim of these shared lessons is to extend the possibilities for social interaction. In future, the school will be looking to drama, art and music to extend social interaction, but this will require changes to the timetable. Staff in resourced provision are trying to make these arrangements but, as one of them commented, 'Sometimes it feels like a school within a school'. Because of the large number of students identified as having special needs there is also concern that the school will be seen as a special school with some mainstream provision. As one teacher stated, 'The difficulty is where does SEN start and finish? The vast majority of kids in school have some form of SEN, where do we make the cut off? Who decides whether a kid has special needs or not?'.

In addition to the resourced provision rooms, there are specially equipped facilities for the small number of students who receive physiotherapy and speech therapy, but it is felt by the SENCO and other staff that there is insufficient support for children with therapy needs. In addition, the school has to cope with a lack of dedicated space that would be required for the development of a wider range of provision; for example, there is a shortage of small teaching rooms, inadequate resources for the visually impaired and insufficient storage space for specialist equipment.

In addition to the resourced provision base, students identified as having special needs in KS3 are in a separate base for most of the time but all spend about a fifth of the week in mainstream classes. KS4 students are supported in mainstream classes and go out of lessons for specialist support.

As can be seen, the school provides a range of options for students who are seen as having special educational needs. At this point in the development of the school's inclusive practices, much of it is in separate classrooms.

Access to the curriculum

Currently, inclusion is conceptualised in terms of access to an appropriate curriculum and the sharing of resources and facilities, as opposed to all students being in mainstream classes all the time. The head of resourced provision pointed out that:

> In this school the number of pupils with SEN means that the standard curriculum is not suitable for many. We should also be re-examining the suitability of that curriculum and its flexibility and have started to do this for Year 7. We have a wide range of special needs but in many cases the range of strategies needed to meet their needs are similar. In the past there was no real curriculum on offer for these pupils.

Several staff commented that many of the students do not have sufficient literacy skills to cope with the mainstream secondary curriculum. According to a senior member of staff,

> One quarter of the pupils can access the curriculum, one quarter can access the curriculum with the extra help we can provide, one quarter can't access the curriculum because we cannot provide the necessary extra help, and the final quarter can't access the curriculum because it's inappropriate.

There is a strong view that the curriculum needs to be changed for many students. For the SENCO, the problem is the lack of an appropriate curriculum to meet students' needs. He explained that a central question being tackled by the school is, 'What is an appropriate curriculum and how do we ensure access for any given group of pupils?'.

Members of the senior management team are committed to the ideal of an inclusive curriculum and the deputy head (curriculum) and the SENCO are working on a new curriculum model which has language and communication at its heart. Central to this re-articulation is to develop an understanding of the concept of language. There are two approaches to this task. The SENCO is looking at students with pre-intentional communication and how this might develop into formal academic language sufficient to access the curriculum. The deputy head is looking at curriculum levels and seeing if the two can be matched. They hope to arrive at the same point but they are coming from different places. An important aspect of this involves the analysis of cross-curricular skills and different subjects and levels of language and communication. They believe that if they can get cross-curricular skills right, then they can get knowledge and content right. One way to understand this is to see it as the removal of barriers to access and the development of a qualitatively different culture. The school is trying to find a way to articulate this task. The SENCO stated, 'We're lucky we have good middle managers who are working hard on this task'.

The senior management team is trying to develop a school-based curriculum-led response to the difficulties faced by many students, but the team acknowledges there is much work still to be done. The SENCO sees this challenge as very exciting: 'Frankly it's why I stay in this school – the work we're doing is really exciting. We were not able to do this before because the curriculum structures were too rigid'.

A number of other initiatives are in place. For example, additional support for literacy is provided through a range of interventions such as an established literacy pull-out programme taught by assistants overseen by teachers. This is an old literacy programme (NFER scheme, National Foundation for Educational Research) and is not part of the learning support department's provision. In this intervention, literacy is seen as an isolated skill and any gains that are apparent in Years 7 and 8 are not sustained and by Year 9 the students drop back. This scheme is described by the SENCO as being dislocated from the curriculum: 'Lots of pupils are still in remediation mode, but we are trying to get them into curriculum mode'.

At the heart of the school's efforts to become more inclusive is the radical review of the curriculum mentioned earlier. According to the SENCO:

> We are including all kids in curriculum but curriculum is widely defined, as developed by Harbour. We have decided not to extend national curriculum downwards but to try and do more than that. The subject boundaries of the curriculum are fine but can become too reductionist.

A major question facing the school relates to the usefulness of schemes intended to make the curriculum more accessible to more children. For example, there are real concerns among middle managers about the *ad hoc* use of approaches such as Performance Indicators for Value Added Target Setting (PIVATS). Curriculum accessibility needs to be seen as a school development task rather than something that individuals develop alone. In thinking about how provision fits together, the SENCO pointed out that 'Originally these pupils were sitting at the side of the class with support but they were not accessing the curriculum; part of how we work together is by having a degree of separation until the curriculum is sorted out'. The long-term plan is to move towards co-location and a more relevant and flexible curriculum.

The organisation of provision for students identified as having special educational needs is complex and reflects the wide range of needs that are catered for in the school. Although the local authority is categorical when writing statements, the curriculum is not categorically led. According to the deputy head:

> The local authority inclusion policy is not working as well as it might in secondary schools that have resourced provision because it is conceptualised categorically and is not defined by curriculum and teaching needs.

The school is working towards taking a curriculum-based approach to meeting the learning needs of all students and the vast majority of students identified as having special educational needs are in mainstream classes full-time. However, it is recognised that many parents start from categorical, deficit-based assumptions (e.g. autism and dyslexia) about their child's difficulties and need to be reassured that their needs will be met. There are demands from some parents and pressure groups for a specialist curriculum for certain 'types' of students. According to the SENCO, 'We cannot operate two systems at once. It's either categorical or a curriculum focus'.

Participation and collaboration: learning together

Students who are part of the resourced provision do not have access to all areas of school life and, indeed, may not need it in some cases. Difficulties include some of the external constraints; for example, although having registration together in the morning would be a good inclusive start to the day, problems with transport make this impossible because students do not arrive until registration is finished.

The extent to which all students are involved in broader aspects of school life varies, and there are different views among staff. According to the assistant SENCO: 'Most pupils have full access to school life and staff are very supportive and try to include pupils in after school activities, except the children who are bussed in'. However, others think that the extent to which those students identified as having profound and multiple learning difficulties mix with other students is variable. Many staff commented that it could be better and that many opportunities are missed. It was pointed out that sports day for students in resourced provision was a separate event and as such was a missed opportunity for sharing an important learning and social occasion. Such aspects of school life are seen as areas for development.

The school has a mixture of provision, some of which could be described as a traditional special education approach. In part this is because it has to cater for students with profound and multiple learning difficulties, but also because there is the belief that students arrive in the school with very low levels of literacy which require targeted support outside the mainstream curriculum.

The school is attempting to reconfigure provision to meet the educational and social needs of its diverse community. There are those who would like to get rid of the concept of special educational needs altogether and focus on curriculum development. Further, many key staff in the school are trying to move away from a categorical conceptualisation of 'special educational needs' and to leave behind simple descriptions of levels of need such as 'school action' or 'school action plus'. However, there are others who find a system of categorisation linked to the 'levels' of intervention, as described in the *Code of Practice* (DfES, 2001b), helpful because it not only provides a language that is widely understood, but also recognises the need for external help from local authority central support services for certain children.

Evidence of achievement

In the most recent inspection, the school was reported as providing satisfactory standards of education in relation to the prior attainment of students. Its levels of achievement, as indicated by progress, are lower than average for the LA (see Table 7.2), although normal for schools with this kind of intake nationally.

The school claims that the Key Stage 2 results in the local feeder primary schools consistently overestimate the attainment levels of students on entry to the school. In the words of the SENCO, 'I don't care what KS2 results say, some kids are functionally illiterate'. Progress at KS3 would appear to be poor, but in the words of one member of the senior management team:

> The apparent key stage two to three dip in attainment is artificial. It is a consequence of the unrealistically high Key Stage 2 results. How can we show progress at Key Stage 3 when children arrive at the school with Key Stage 2 results that over estimate their attainment? And because the requirements at key stage two and three are totally different, it is difficult to measure progress reliably.

Several staff commented that students learning English as an additional language are less likely to have inflated Key Stage 2 results because they are more likely to have difficulty with the tests. These lower scores when they are younger mean there is more scope for improvement later in their school careers. But there was also a widespread view amongst some staff that poor achievement was more likely to be associated with low aspirations and lack of support for learning at home. As one teacher explained:

> Working class English kids in this school are the majority and they don't have access to books at home. It's only one explanation, but KS2 SATs results for non-native speakers are not inflated so progress is seen.

GCSE results are below the national and local authority average although they are on a par with the three comparison mixed comprehensive schools which have lower numbers of pupils designated as having special needs (see Table 7.3).

Further, Ofsted see achievement levels in the school as satisfactory given the real starting points of many of the students on entering the school and the high levels of mobility. Significant numbers of Year 11 students did not start the school in Year 7, although these numbers are lower than the LA average.

Table 7.2   Mean achievement statistics for Harbour School and the whole LA, 2003

LA	*All students*	*Non SEN (n=2035)*	*SEN (n=413)*
KS2 average pts	24.2	24.9	20.7
GCSECAP points	36.7	39.7	22.0
Harbour School	*All students*	*Non SEN (n=97)*	*SEN (n=71)*
KS2 average pts	24.4	25.3	23.3
GCSECAP points	24.7	26.7	21.8

Table 7.3   Harbour School and three comparison schools in the LA with lower percentage of students identified as having SEN, 2005

	Harbour School	Comparison schools (average)
Number of students at the end of KS4	205	227
Number of KS4 students with SEN with statements	6	7
Percentage of KS4 students with SEN with statements	2.9%	3.0%
Number of KS4 students with SEN without statements	94	17
Percentage of KS4 students with SEN without statements	45.9%	7.23%
Percentage of students achieving Level 2 (5 or more grades A*–C)	35%	35%
Percentage of students achieving Level 1 (5 or more grades A*–G)	88%	90.3%
Percentage of students achieving at least one qualification	97%	96.66%
Average total point score per student	278.7	291

Recognition and acceptance

Some students designated as having special needs do have social contact with their peers and have other students who 'look out for them' in lessons. For some there is good social interaction. As one member of staff pointed out: 'Some SEN kids stick together but some can cope with the social side of being in a big school. Children are OK with each other here. Attitudes are nice'. It is clear that friendships between students in resourced provision and elsewhere in the school do exist and there is a sense of tolerance and acceptance: 'Kids mix with a wider circle. This is helped when they are from the local catchment area and they meet outside school'.

Nevertheless students from resourced provision tend to stick together because support workers are constantly with them at lunchtime and natural opportunities for social contact are not necessarily easy. The attitudes of other students have not always been good. As a teacher in the resourced provision stated, 'A kid knocked on door and said, "Is this the disabled class?" I made him come into the lesson and do work and asked him what he learned, and he wanted to come back'.

Such separation and suspicion is not only true for the students. Some staff distinguish between students. According to a learning support teacher, 'I think they make a distinction – your kids and our kids. There is a danger of shifting a line where more kids become pathologised. Our department shifts the line back'. She went on to suggest that making separate provision for some students had an impact on teachers' thinking elsewhere in the school. As she pointed out, some colleagues might suggest, 'You are the experts on SEN, why don't you deal with all of them, especially behaviour difficulties?'. There is pressure from some teachers for members of the learning support department to deal with behaviour difficulties and the problems they have with classroom management.

Issues raised by the discussion

Funding and budgets

The school budget is managed as a whole but the resourced provision allowance is spent only on those students for whom it is specifically designated. There is a £1 million budget to operate learning support as the SENCO sees fit. According to the SENCO the local authority is unaware of how much the school's budget subsidises provision for students designated as having special educational needs. With such large numbers of students so identified, the budget is insufficient. However, it is unclear whether the budget consists only of the additional designated funding or whether it also includes the basic per capita funding that is allocated for all students.

In recent years the local authority has uncoupled funding from a needs-based formula in an attempt to reduce the demand for statementing. It is moving towards a cluster moderation system in which groups of schools share funding according to agreed procedures. The main mechanism consists of meetings at which heads or SENCOs make bids for additional funding. The bids are then evaluated and the meeting decides who and what should be funded. The SENCO thinks this arrangement is a good idea, as it is an attempt to be more open and transparent but he argues that it is not working as well as it might, partly because the criteria are not clear and also because some SENCOs are more persuasive than others. He pointed out that a medical referral was always more likely to be successful in securing additional resources, but it may not be more accurate, or educationally relevant. There is also insufficient understanding of the needs of students with degenerative conditions, which may eventually be terminal. In such cases, other students, parents and staff, as well as the individual students themselves, also need support.

The school is trying to blur the boundaries between resourced provision, students with statements and the mainstream, but feel that the local authority has not yet caught up with the school and the delegated budget process is not yet sufficiently responsive.

Curriculum and assessment

As previously mentioned there has been a major focus on developing a more relevant and appropriate curriculum for all children in the school. In addition there is also the Year 7 project that is co-ordinated by the KS3 strategy manager. The project attempts to incorporate aspects of good primary practice into Year 7. Students now spend more time with fewer teachers so that the school day is less disjointed. There is widespread support for the social benefits of the project but some subject specialists regret the reduction in time spent learning their subject and worry about some teachers' lack of knowledge about subject content. Some are concerned that the students will not have a good grounding in their subjects. These major curriculum initiatives reflect a widespread belief that the national curriculum does not meet the learning needs of many students in the school.

Assessment presents particular challenges for the school. There are two elements to this; the first relates to the identification and assessment of children's needs and the second is concerned with how best to assess children's progress. According to the SENCO, some staff are too keen to ask for external assessment rather than carry out some of the basic assessment themselves. This is partly because of a lack of expertise, experience and confidence. Training is therefore a major professional development issue for all staff. The school is gradually trying to build up this expertise so that assessment is related to the curriculum and is able to provide evidence of children's learning.

As previously mentioned, the school considers the primary schools' assessment of special needs and the results of Key Stage 2 SATs to be unreliable. Therefore, according to the Key Stage 3 manager:

> We do a lot of assessment at year seven to check children's starting points and there is a disparity between pupils' scores and standardised reading assessments. About a third of our pupils are not able to access the secondary curriculum at all and 50 per cent find it challenging. We are starting year seven pupils on a more primary curriculum model with a strong focus on literacy.

All provision in the school is evaluated but a senior member of staff suggested that this is not well established yet nor is it sufficiently effective. There is a team that monitors provision and they are developing a training programme that will enable colleagues to judge whether they are meeting needs and whether students are making progress, not just checking what is in place.

The development of staff expertise in assessment for learning as well as the assessment of learning lies at the heart of improving inclusion and achievement. Without good evidence of inclusion and achievement it is difficult to bring about improvements in practice.

Staff expertise

Generally there is commitment to students who have been identified with special educational needs, including those who are part of the resourced provision, but many staff across the school feel they lack knowledge and expertise. With increasing delegation of funding and a reduction in local authority central support services, the school needs to develop on-site specialism but this is constrained by the turnover of staff. Lack of stable experienced staffing is a major problem. Recruitment of staff to the resourced provision is relatively easy compared to the rest of the school. Because of difficulties with recruitment and retention of staff, many overseas teachers are appointed. Senior management of the school suggest that these teachers have much to offer, but they need additional training, not only to work in the English system, but also to meet the diverse range of needs that exist in the student population. In addition, senior staff see the need to develop a range of skills amongst staff as a whole, including more effective classroom management and organisation skills, and a better notion of differentiation. The school funds such training but the 20 per cent turnover of staff means there is a continuing need which is hard to meet. According to the head, the local authority needs to develop a strategy to make the area more attractive to teachers, not only so that recruitment is easier but also to ensure that teachers stay in their jobs.

Staff development is seen as crucial and the school is committed to growing its own expertise. The school has negotiated an advanced diploma with a local university that is tutored in part by the SENCO, who described training as 'the only way we can sustain what we are doing'. Some other external courses are seen as good for raising awareness but do not give the necessary practical skills. In an attempt to provide such skills the local authority has based an advisory teacher in the school for a day a week to develop and train staff 'on the job'. According to the SENCO things are moving forward and this training fits really well with the school's present needs and organisational structure. Nevertheless, the headteacher feels the school needs more advisory support from specialists particularly in the area of communication skills including sign language and in dealing with violent behaviour.

The staff development programme has two elements. First, there is training for the special needs staff. Teachers in the resourced provision base have after-school training every Thursday and other staff are welcome to attend. Other members of the learning support department receive professional development in specific forms of special educational needs and pedagogical matters and also in the skills of consultancy, sharing expertise and working in partnership with colleagues.

Second, there is training for the rest of the school staff on issues such as curriculum-based assessment, working with Individual Education Plans (IEPs) and differentiation. The head feels that all training should be consistent with the priorities identified in the school development plan. An example of this is that members of the local authority multi-sensory support team are working with the school in focusing on priorities identified by staff. Much of the responsibility for staff development rests with a few members of staff with limited support from the local authority.

Expectations

In discussions with several staff it became clear that some teachers and assistants see many of the problems faced by students as a reflection of beliefs about, and perceptions of, the local community. The area is described as being a predominantly white working class community, with severe poverty, high levels of crime, disrupted family life, low levels of literacy skills, low levels of aspiration and high mobility. One teacher stated, 'We don't have many aspirational Asian families at this school who are ambitious for their children. We have the white working class parents who didn't have the skills to escape from this area'. Although not all teachers share these views, it explains to some extent the low expectations of some of the staff, which, according to a member of the school's senior management team, are communicated to the students. The consequence is that many children do not expect to do well in school, nor do they see school as particularly relevant to them and their lives. A major task for senior management in the school is to raise expectations of the staff and aspirations of the students.

Links with external agencies

With increasing delegation of resources and a reduction in the nature and extent of central services provided by the local authority, all schools in the authority have to develop their own expertise. Considerable expertise left the borough when the learning support service was disbanded and the budget was delegated. As the headteacher pointed out, 'Centrally held services have been decimated so we are needing to build in-house specialism and this is a long-term project'.

The school does not use local authority central services except in the area of visual impairment where they do not have the expertise. Otherwise the school is developing the same levels of expertise as people from central services. According to the SENCO, the problem has been that the central services are still categorical (speech and language, social, emotional and behavioural difficulties and so forth) not curriculum-led.

> We need a service which supports the schools and is accountable to the students rather than upwards to the authority monitoring structures. With the reduction of statutory assessments psychologists should have more time to support schools. Currently the educational psychology service is insufficient to support the school's needs, but those we do have working with us are good.

The speech and language service has good expertise but some staff are currently on leave and there has been no replacement. Physiotherapist support is good. Occupational therapists are unavailable. If the school could get staff skills to a higher level, then external therapists could diagnose students' problems and suggest the kind of support needed and staff could provide it. The school is working to develop such skills in-house, but it takes time.

According to the headteacher:

> The local authority lacks a holistic plan for inclusion. The special needs service and administration is fine, but they are separate and not incorporated into other authority services. Other authority agencies seem to go on separately from special needs.

Senior staff in the school suggested that the local authority school support agencies need to be part of an overall inclusive approach and be more collaborative. This would include support for some of the practical problems such as links at transfer from primary school, transport and encouraging sharing specialist provision between schools.

The head pointed out that many children in the school have chronic health problems that have an impact on their education. To help overcome these problems, better links between health and education agencies were required. In turn such contacts would help parents to negotiate their way through the complex process of getting support for their children. The school has been working hard to improve communication with many parents and it is now felt to be satisfactory. In particular, staff from the resourced provision have good personal contact with parents. It is less so with those who work with other students who have been identified as having special educational needs. The SENCO feels more needs to be done and contact with families could be developed further.

Inclusion and achievement

Much of the additional support available in the school is targeted on students in resourced provision and on those other students with statements. Levels of achievement for students described as having special educational needs are similar to the local authority average. Other interventions may not be so successful, for example, literacy interventions are described as being disconnected from the curriculum. Many teachers state that poor levels of literacy impede some students' understanding of much of the subject content necessary to achieve higher grades at GCSE. Clearly there is further work still to be done on the development of a coherent system that is able to support learning across the curriculum.

It is interesting to note that the levels of achievement at GCSE/GNVQ are lower than the local authority average, which includes the results from secondary schools that do not have open admissions policies (see Table 7.2). However, results from Harbour are on a par with three comparison schools in the LA which have significantly lower proportions of pupils thought to have special needs (see Table 7.3).

Although the attitudes of many staff are positive, others feel that those students who have been identified as having complex special needs and/or behaviour difficulties should not be in the school. Further, some teachers have low expectations of the students because of their perceptions of the community and the problems that it faces. In turn these low expectations are associated with low aspirations.

The school faces major challenges in its attempts to develop approaches that are inclusive and also raise standards of achievement because of problems with the recruitment and retention of suitably qualified teachers.

Questions could be asked about the extent to which the school is inclusive. There is extensive separate provision within the school and according to many staff many opportunities to bring together students across the school are missed. Further, there are those who claim that the impact of having so much segregated, 'special' provision in the school results in many teachers seeing the 'special needs task' as a problem to be dealt with by other people, preferably in a different place. However, it may also be argued that this is an essential stage in the school's evolution as an inclusive school given the nature and extent of the difficulties it faces.

Table 7.4   Value-added measures 2005

KS2 to KS4 Value-added	
KS2–KS4 value-added measure	943.0
Percentage of students at the end of KS4 included in VA calculation	90%
Average number of qualifications (equiv. to GCSE) taken by KS2–KS4 VA students	9.2
KS3 to KS4 Value-added	
KS3–KS4 value-added measure	993.1
Percentage of students included in KS3–KS4 VA calculation	95%

Harbour School faces many of the challenges of schools serving similar communities. Given the close relationship between attainment and special needs status it is not surprising that the school has the highest percentage of students identified as having special needs in the authority (see Tables 7.1 and 7.3) and is also one of the lowest performing (see Table 7.2). Yet if the results of Key Stage 2 tests are to be believed, levels of attainment on entry to the school at age 11 are near the authority average (see Table 7.2). As previously mentioned there are a number of possible explanations for this phenomenon. In particular the Key Stage 2 results may be an overestimation of students' true level of attainment on entry to the school. This then limits the scope for the school to demonstrate 'value-added' during Key Stage 3 (see Table 7.4). In an attempt to address this apparent underachievement the school has embarked upon a radical review of the curriculum, which may lead to improved teaching and learning in the long-term.

Harbour is a school that is doing many things well. It is undertaking a significant review of its curriculum and assessment policies and practices and has made real progress in developing staff expertise. It provides a valuable resource to an impoverished community. For many children living in difficult circumstances, it provides the best hope they have for a better future.

8 Chester Community School

Introduction

Chester Community School is a co-educational 11 to 16 comprehensive school that serves an area of severe deprivation. The school is located in a community where the percentage of students across the school eligible for free school meals (FSM) is around 50 per cent, well above the national average. English is an additional language for over three-quarters of the school's population and many different ethnic communities are represented in the school. Over one quarter of the students are identified as having special educational needs (see Table 8.1). The attainment of students on entry is slightly below the local authority (LA) average, which means that it is well below the national average; however, a recent Ofsted report describes the school as having high achievement given the starting point of its students and the population it serves (see Tables 8.2 and 8.4). The school faces a number of challenging circumstances such as difficulties in recruitment and retention of teachers and relatively high levels of student mobility.

In this school, responses to students who experience difficulties in learning are part of senior management responsibility. There is a faculty of social inclusion organised into five departments working across the school to develop inclusion and reduce exclusion. The school has additional resources to support deaf students and others whose learning difficulties require exceptional levels of resourcing. The school has used the additional resources that having a high proportion of students identified as having special educational needs brings in innovative ways to support the learning of all students across the curriculum.

Evidence of inclusion and links to achievement

Participation and access: being there

Chester Community School is a large comprehensive secondary school (n=1,300) offering places to students aged 11 to 16 from linked primary schools and those whose parents have named a preference for the school. Priority is given to children who have a brother or sister already enrolled in the school and those who live closest to the preferred school. At the time of the case study nearly 5 per cent of students had a statement of special educational needs, while one-third of students (30.4 per cent) were considered to have some kind of special educational need.

The school describes itself as an inclusive school in its mission statement and it has developed admission, attendance and exclusion policies as well as a code of conduct in line with this ethos. As one member of staff summed it up:

> Students start at Year 7. Everyone is worried, then kids settle in and by the end of the year they have been integrated into lessons. But it is still a big job to enable teachers to feel they can teach/support these pupils.

The school operates a five one hour period timetable between the hours of 8.25 a.m. and 3.00 p.m. with tutor time and assembly at the end of the day. The school reported 93 per cent attendance during 2002–3 despite a high degree of student mobility (staff report between 5 and 10 per cent in any one year group). Unauthorised absences are monitored very carefully and this is a key administrative task. The school has very good data on who is truanting from which lessons. Truancy is considered a problem for a small group of Year 10 and Year 11 students who feel disenfranchised; some have low literacy levels but emotional and behavioural difficulties are thought to be the main problem. Ofsted rated the school as satisfactory on attendance and behaviour, including the extent of exclusions. However, staff interviewed for this study held themselves to a higher standard and spoke of their reluctance to exclude and their disappointment with a recent decision to permanently exclude three students. As one member of staff noted: 'Exclusion is not only on the agenda but cannot be removed – the question is how to prevent it from happening'.

Chester's Code of Conduct includes an anti-bullying policy. It encourages respect for others and safety. Ofsted rated the school as good overall on students' attitudes, values and other personal qualities. The report noted that

> the school has much to offer its students … the strong network of support of all students instils confidence, which manifests itself in an enthusiasm for school and for learning. Students feel trusted and consider the school takes an interest in their views.

The strong network of support the school operates has its nexus in social inclusion. There is an assistant headteacher for social inclusion whose area of responsibility is to oversee the support of all students in mainstream subjects including those with additional learning and behavioural needs. A social inclusion faculty is the largest department in the school, with 50 to 60 members of staff. Students identified as having special educational needs receive support through a combination of in-class support, individual tuition and small group literacy work. There is a base unit for students with hearing impairments (deaf support department), a learning support department and a student support centre located within the school where students are timetabled for lessons and from where additional support in mainstream lessons is managed. The school gets additional funding to support some of these activities from a range of national initiatives.

The school is welcoming of students from a variety of cultural backgrounds and some members of staff are fluent in British Sign Language (BSL) and some speak Urdu, Bengali, Somali, Arabic, Gujerati, French and Spanish. As a result families who do not speak English often can communicate with the school. As a 'Full Service School', Chester offers courses for children and adults in the evenings, at weekends and during school holidays. It also provides a one-stop advice centre for health and other services. Chester has links with the wider community ranging from the local theatre and youth action projects to the local sixth form college. Students in the school are involved in organising celebrations around religious and cultural festivals. Though theft is an issue for the school, necessitating some areas to be locked, this barrier to access belies a substantial commitment to and level of community involvement.

Children with physical disabilities are welcome in the school although full physical access is problematic. Recent building work has brought some improvements, though the new security doors do not stay open for wheelchairs to pass through. Though the physical space allocated to the learning support department has improved in recent years, it is not accessible to students with physical disabilities because the main part of the department is upstairs and pressures of limited space have made it impossible to move. According to one senior member of staff, the cost to renovate the school to make it fully accessible was quoted at £10 million, well beyond the capacity of the school to undertake. The new reception area, however, is physically accessible and children with physical disabilities were observed to be included in games in the playground. While the reception area does not yet have anyone who signs and there are sometimes problems in remembering that school trips must have staff who can sign in order for students with hearing impairments to be included, staff in the school do not defend or justify barriers to inclusion. As one member of staff said: 'Whenever a decision is taken, the first question has to be "What are the implications for inclusion?" The DDA is beginning to help us in developing access policy'. Another said: 'The strength of the school is that we are a responsive school. We evolve with the needs of the students'.

The head of the social inclusion faculty has led the school in the development of a new inclusion policy which aims to bring the Special Needs and English as an Additional Language departments closer together. For example, rather than keeping a 'special needs register', the school keeps an 'additional needs register', which is intended to enable provision mapping exercises to be undertaken for all students with additional needs, including refugee children. There are structures in place for termly meetings between directors of studies and the social inclusion faculty to discuss the status of students with additional needs and to develop action plans.

Access to the wider curriculum is open to all students. There is a range of extra curricular provision including break and lunchtime support, homework clubs and field trips. Of particular note is that access to the wider curriculum is not restricted to any one group of students. As one of the staff interviewed for this study noted: 'It's nice here – lots of hearing kids learn sign, they can do GCSE sign or lunch club'. Two deaf instructors teach BSL to hearing students and staff. In this way access to the wider curriculum is not just about students with special educational needs but all students.

Participation and collaboration: learning together

Two interrelated topics are of particular importance here: one has to do with support for teaching and learning (including teacher–student and teacher–teacher support); the second with participation in assessment tasks. Each of these is discussed separately below.

The learning support department within the school employs a team of 25 staff including 18 full-time learning support assistants (LSAs). There has been a rapid expansion of this department over the past three years and staff turnover among LSAs has been high. A number of strategies have been put in place to stabilise the staff mainly through induction and professional development. For example, LSAs are required to obtain City and Guilds qualifications within two years of appointment. In exchange they are paid more than they would be at other area schools in the local authority.

In addition to a large team of LSAs, there are four learning support teachers, a KS4 and assessment co-ordinator, a KS3 and exceptional resources team manager and a head of department. Although each member of staff has discrete role responsibilities, the structure is designed for maximum flexibility in catering for a wide range of student needs and in supporting curriculum development across the school. For example, the growth of the learning support department has enabled the deployment of LSAs to subject departments. The aim of this model of learning support is to achieve good management systems: a network of support across the curriculum rather than one person supporting one student only all day. There is a view within the school that having LSAs in departments raises attainment for all students. As one member of staff put it: 'These kids [with SEN] cause concerns at first but the extra support that comes into the school helps the mainstream kids too'.

The LSAs are managed by the head of the learning support department and they meet together once a week to review their work. They also attend department meetings in their subject area. The head of learning support views this model of learning support as one that is supportive of curriculum development within the school. Subject teachers are seen as specialists in subject learning but members of the learning support department are specialists with respect to individual needs. Though LSAs are assigned to faculties, they support students in need of exceptional resources. The aim is to match individual need to the demands of the subject curriculum. Individual Education Plans (IEPs) are used to provide teachers with an overview of additional needs and up to three targets are updated weekly. This is seen as good practice but considered by some staff from the learning support department as being unrealistic. However, the deployment of

LSAs to departments has been a huge success according to a number of staff interviewed.

Though one team of LSAs is assigned to subject departments, the learning support department also operates a base room where students can divide their time between lessons and individual support. There is a recognition that some children, with more complex needs, require one to one support. As a result there is a team of exceptional resource LSAs who follow the child instead of the curriculum area. There is also an issue of access to the national curriculum for students working below level one. The learning support department conceptualises access in terms of the development of a parallel curriculum joined by topic areas. However, all 'withdrawal' from mainstream is aimed at increasing access to the mainstream curriculum. This was described by one member of staff as follows: 'Year seven work can be done/adapted at level one. Year 11 cannot. Need to work towards something. ASDAN [Award Scheme Development and Accreditation Network] needs to be linked to subject topic – don't want to pull out programme'.

Assessment of students' attainment is an important issue for the school and as students move through the curriculum an increasing emphasis (particularly at KS4) is placed on 'getting students through exams'. Until recently, all students identified with special educational needs have been entered for exams and the KS4 and assessment co-ordinator has responsibility for special entry for examinations. Staff encourage students to take as many GCSE (General Certificate of Secondary Education) exams as possible, but there is an awareness that some students will not take examinations and a concern about what should be done for them instead. Again the theme of a parallel curriculum was discussed: 'We need a parallel curriculum for kids who cannot participate in or access the national curriculum. We need ASDAN, life skills curriculum, but we also need to recognise that they can access some parts of the [main] curriculum, such as the Arts'.

For students identified as having special educational needs progress is also monitored through the annual review process. As the school has included more students with severe learning difficulties there is a need to offer a more differentiated curriculum. Moreover, these students are not entered for examinations. However, this does not mean the school has failed to include them in assessment tasks. Instead the school has initiated a curriculum project to develop schemes of work and alternative qualifications such as ASDAN that are more differentiated so that the needs of a greater range of students can be accommodated.

As part of the management team of the department, the KS3 co-ordinator is responsible for the transition of students from Year 6 to Year 7; whereas the KS4 Co-ordinator is responsible for the transition from Year 11. These postholders also have responsibility for students who require exceptional resources and special examination requirements respectively. In this way the management team share responsibility for all students with additional needs and liaises with heads of subject departments to ensure that students receive the correct levels of support.

In addition it is possible for the school to apply for additional resources from the LA. For example, a case might be made for funding for a link course for one or two students. There are approximately 500 students at KS4 at any given time, and, of these, 30 to 40 are considered to be 'disaffected students' who need mixed provision. This was described as two days in school for literacy and three days work/apprenticeship in college or the community. In such cases, students stay on the school roll but staff admitted to looking for ways to avoid counting them in exam returns. Staff also said there was some pressure to 'play a numbers game' with the examination returns so as to present the school in the best possible light. And, as one member of staff put it:

> We are doing a reasonable job but there is still a huge drop out … when you look at who goes to [alternative provision], on the one hand, kids are getting a better curriculum (presumably), but on the other hand kids have been written off. How can we say we're doing better?

However, the prevailing view is that virtually everyone on the roll takes GCSE examinations. The perception is that the school 'probably loses 1–2 per cent'. In other words, up to 5 out of 270 students are likely to be enrolled in Education Otherwise provision and will not take any GCSEs at Chester, and a few others 'vote with their feet' by not attending school. The view was expressed that at age 16 there is not much anyone can do if the students opt out. Still, there was agreement that students do not like being excluded from exams and feel it is unjust when this happens. Some staff felt strongly that every student should have the chance to do mock exams, as exclusion from this exercise gives the message that the student is failing. There is a debate within the school about who decides who is entered for exams and who is not.

When GCSE results are published the school undertakes an analysis of performance of students designated as having special educational needs by subject area. The interview with the member of staff responsible for special entry suggested that about four or five students per year get amanuensis. This is in addition to extra time that is permitted without special accommodations; however, staff do not encourage this option and very few students are considered to require it. The view among staff is that if a student cannot do the exam, extra time will not help. Some students are seen to need an alternative way to demonstrate what they know but staff are concerned that alternative arrangements must be fair. Extra time was seen as not always fair. Alternative special examination arrangements on the other hand are not considered extra help. This was summed up as: 'The student with A to C knowledge but F to G performance needs alternative assessment. These students need opportunity to demonstrate knowledge. This is not "help"'.

The issue of fairness was raised with respect to examination conditions for deaf students. Special exam arrangements have been requested for such students but staff reported that the examination board Edexcel did not always respond to requests for up to 25 per cent more time and signing questions. Moreover, in English students are not able to have signed questions, as reading is part of the assessment, and so in this subject only directions can be signed. As the head of the department pointed out, there is a need to find ways of explaining to the examination board that this is linguistically biased.

Staff involved in learning support identified the understanding of subject teachers about the achievement of students at lower levels of attainment as important. All departments now comment on exam statistics and this is seen as an important step forward as departments need to interpret statistics and use this information in their subsequent curriculum planning (e.g. using target setting to track the progress of students identified as having special educational needs). Work on the KS3 curriculum was cited in response to the KS3 dip in test results, although some staff do believe this dip has been exaggerated. Nevertheless the school has focused on raising achievement at KS3 through the delegation of LSAs to subject departments and at KS4 through the development of alternative accreditation schemes.

Supporting students to work together can be viewed through the lens of student voices about their experience at Chester. In an interview with a Year 10 student who is supported by the student support centre, the concept of inclusion was articulated in the identification of the school as a community school:

> I like it that it is a community school – not like xxxx school. They can reject you or they limit you. This school takes everyone – there are a lot of deaf kids. I like the homework club and after-school clubs. Lots of sports here. I like football and play for the school. I always go to xxxx to see football. I'm good at music and graphics. I would take IT but it takes up two options. I'm doing five or six GCSEs: Maths, English, Science, Drama, Graphics and Music. My Dad is pushing me to get a full education because if you get an education you can help yourself and help the family back home. Also, my Dad never had an education.

Rather than perceiving the student support centre as a form of exclusion within the school, students found it a supportive place. As another student put it:

> Chester is good – if you have behaviour problems you can come to xxxx and they sort it. If you have temper problems like me, they work on telling you how to avoid problems – like walk away or take a deep breath.
>
> In here teachers give one-to-one so you get better learning and teachers teach properly. I'll get better GCSEs down here, because teachers are not working with 30 kids.
>
> I'm learning how to get along with people. I'm learning to own my own behaviour and if I get told off, then I say I'm sorry. I used to walk out. My problems started in the nursery when I put sand in another kid's mouth.

In response to a question about whether or not he worried about exclusion, another student said:

> Last year I didn't take secondary school seriously. My uncle was like me. In a way history is repeating itself. All my friends without an education don't have very good jobs but my uncle sorted himself out and he is a financial

consultant for Barclays in the City. With my mum and dad I made a plan for my future. I want a proper education and to get a good future.

The head of the student support centre described Chester as much better than a lot of schools because the head and SMT, and the school ethos, are quite sympathetic to the needs of troubled students.

> When I came here all statemented kids were in all lessons but in reality very little differentiation was going on and teachers were happy when kids were absent. It was very difficult going into different subjects to support students. There was some informal co-teaching. When I came it was part of Excellence in Cities. I was part of Central Services. The head twisted my arm to stay and set up the Centre – he was very clear it was not to be a dumping ground – though some staff thought we were getting our own loony bin – but the head countered this. Now we're seen as OK because we get results – decreasing exclusions.

Participation and diversity: recognition and acceptance

Perhaps the most interesting aspect of Chester's commitment to inclusion can be found in the policies and practices that support deaf students in the school. Over 20 years ago, the LA undertook to close its specialist provision in favour of a model of resourced provision in which particular mainstream schools were given additional resources to help them meet the needs of students who would otherwise attend special schools. Greenway Primary School, a feeder school to Chester, established resourced provision for deaf and partially hearing students and over time, as students moved through the primary years, provision was established at Chester so that as students left Greenway they could move with their peer group to secondary school. Over the past six years provision at Chester has grown from three students in Year 7 to 20 students across all year groups.

The head of the department described a policy of inclusion based on the belief that deaf students need access to qualified subject teachers, not teachers of the deaf who have an A-level in a particular subject. In practice this has meant that deaf students are timetabled for classes in the mainstream but staff from the department support them. There are 15 staff in the department: nine communicators, two deaf instructors, two teachers of the deaf, one deaf LSA and one administrator. Communicators are qualified communication support workers who sign lessons so that deaf students can have access to the mainstream curriculum. For example, during a Year 9 maths lesson on radius, diameter and circumference, students worked independently at tables in groups of five. The communicator stood at the front of the class signing and interpreting teacher and student talk. The casual observer would not have been able to identify the deaf student except when the communicator made eye contact with the student and went over to help work out a problem. Or when the deaf student answered one of the teacher's questions and the communicator interpreted. At another point during the lesson when the teacher was checking students' work, the communicator served as a link – monitoring student eye contact and giving a thumbs up for completed problems. When the teacher asked for answers, deaf students raised their hands and it became apparent that there was more than one deaf student in the classroom.

During the interview with the communicator after the lesson observation, it was revealed that the two deaf students in the lesson did not have additional special educational needs. The communicator noted that these students could keep up with the work but that some students need more input. She felt the system of supporting all students with hearing impairments in mainstream classes worked for some but not all students. For example, deaf students with additional educational needs, such as refugee students, were considered more difficult to support because the difficulties they experienced were more complex. When asked if she was expected to work with all students in the class, the communicator replied that though it was not her specific role to do this, she would help others if appropriate (e.g. if she were not signing during an independent problem solving activity). The head of the department argued that teaching students to know when help is required and when it is not is an important part of the work. She noted that staff feel guilty if they are not signing rather than celebrating that this means the students do not need the help.

Another aim of the department's work is to educate all students about how to communicate with and respond appropriately to people with hearing impairments. To this end British Sign Language is seen as a modern foreign language and all Chester students are encouraged to learn it. Deaf students are encouraged to take on roles of responsibility in the school (e.g. helping with the lunch queue or participating on the student tribunal). There was some concern that these experiences came at a price. For example, when discussing the mainstream experiences of one student, the head of the department said of one student: 'If she went to xxxx [specialist facility] she probably would have got better GCSEs but in fewer subjects and she would have been more protected from the real world'.

This led to a discussion about how one reconciles the issues of inclusion with the issue of deaf culture and identity. In response, the head of the department noted that one deaf adult in a hearing environment is not a good idea: that there is a need for a critical mass of deaf students in the school (hence the rationale for a department). She acknowledged that there was a fear within the deaf community of a dilution of culture, as found for example in the radical idea among some members of the deaf community that cochlear implants are a form of genocide. However, her view was that it is easier to be deaf if you know how the hearing world works:

> We aim to [give] kids skills to live in a deaf and a hearing world. Not one or the other but to move back and forth. Deaf culture is very important. We are not trying to make our kids' hearing [normal] but they can't make informed choices about the world they want to live in without experience of both.

The deaf learning support assistant and two deaf instructors who support deaf students in mainstream subjects and teach BSL to hearing students and staff held a different view. They disagreed with the argument put forward by the head of the department that mainstream school prepares deaf students to move between two worlds. One said:

> I would like the deaf schools to open again. Here there are only 22 kids. We went to deaf school. Today's children are behind – they don't have deaf role models. I feel very sorry for the kids. They are missing what I had at deaf boarding school.
>
> In my day you had to learn English. Got the cane if you signed. Here the level of attainment is not very high. Year 11 pupils ask how to spell 'before' or 'I'.

Another deaf member of staff said she also went to a unit for the deaf that then closed and so she had to go to a mainstream school from Year 9. She felt that time in a specialist unit was a great benefit to her during her years of mainstream education:

> My view is that a lot of people don't really accept deaf people – not enough time given to develop this acceptance. I support children with limited language development who are not always better off in mainstream schools. In deaf schools you're all together. Here teachers give lessons too quickly and communicators can't always keep up.

When asked if there were benefits for deaf students in mainstream schools the deaf members of staff felt the school was accessible but could be better with the infusion of more resources. They argued that classroom teachers often leave things to the communicators, who are not qualified teachers. As one put it: 'Communicators are cheap labour'. They felt there were greater benefits for hearing students who get sign language instruction than deaf children who get communicators rather than qualified teachers who are fluent in sign. Their position is that deaf people at deaf schools are better integrated in the hearing world 'because in deaf school you acquire a sense of identity and pride that is lacking here'. They pointed out that deaf students congregate together and do not really mix with mainstream students. This was supported by other members of staff who agreed that one was more likely to see deaf students with deaf friends rather than with hearing friends or hearing siblings. Hearing students rarely come into the department.

The deaf members of staff argued that deaf students at Chester were lonely and that they were missing opportunities to move into the adult world of the deaf community. Deaf students can have a limited social life. Other staff observed that, like all students, deaf students make new friends in secondary school and like other secondary school students they are looking for a peer group they can identify with, but that this does not negate the importance of schooling in a hearing culture where deaf children are accepted (i.e. hearing students have some BSL).

Deaf students were also circumspect about their experiences. Three Year 10 students interviewed expressed mixed views. When asked about whether hearing students were helpful all three students said yes and no. They said:

> I like design technology. I'm good and I can work really fast. I work on my own. Other boys only sign a little bit and sometimes they are silly. Science is hard. Writing for GCSE is hard.

> A girl helps me in maths – two girls at my table – we talk.

> Sometimes hearing people help me with my writing. I prefer to be with deaf people because it is easier and they can understand.

> In dance hearing girls help me. Some of them sign and I teach them. Maths not really.

The experiences of the students were reflected in the tour of school they gave us where we passed by French and English classes but lingered at dance and drama, art and (fashion) textiles, and photography.

With respect to recognition and acceptance of deaf staff by hearing staff, deaf staff felt that personal relationships were important but that the structure of the school still reinforced a hearing/deaf divide. As one member of staff put it, there is an assumption that the hearing world knows best:

> We go out for drinks on Friday – we teach them deaf awareness. I feel involved – not as much as I want but I feel involved. I'd like more responsibility but they have the last word because they have qualifications, but we have the experience – expertise.

With respect to other areas of staff relations, the overall impression is that these are good and this is supported by Ofsted who found morale within the school to be high. Staff are actively engaged in supporting each other. There is a group that meets informally after school every few weeks to talk about how things are going and to provide support.

Discussion

In an interview for this study, the headteacher noted that there is what he called a paradox with respect to different types of identified special educational needs, social integration, and teaching and learning. That these issues are seen as paradoxical arises in part because of various school structures and different meanings of inclusion.

For example, one member of staff works half the time as a sign language interpreter (communicator) and half the time as a school counsellor. He is moving towards a full-time counselling role where he will become a school counsellor who can sign thereby enabling deaf students to access school counselling services. The student support centre and the learning mentors are supported by different initiatives and work well together although the geography of the school makes it difficult for them to liaise.

The tension between curriculum development and exam performance and accountability is similar to that found in other secondary schools in England, but the organisation of a social inclusion faculty is unique. Though staff struggle with issues of inclusion and exclusion there is a sense of improvement in provision and performance over time. All staff interviewed were reflective about their practice and keen to talk about areas of improvement as well as things they felt they did well. There was a sense that issues of quality were foremost in staff debates. As one member of staff said:

> What is quality provision? What are we doing at Key Stage 4? [The LA] used to 'dump' at this phase. Now a student doesn't turn up, a phone call gets made. A few years ago this would not have happened.

There is ongoing debate within the school about what can be achieved. Provision for students with hearing impairments is considered excellent but staff say there is still a long way to go. Staff debate the merits of including children who have been identified as having other forms of special educational needs, particularly those with severe learning difficulties. Some argue that inclusion means the school should be able to accommodate all who attend the feeder schools even if it is not additionally resourced to make this provision. They feel that success stories help teachers to come around to a more positive view.

In the school, responses to students identified as having special educational needs are part of senior management responsibility and the school has taken advantage of the LA delegation of the special needs budget, and the de-coupling of funding from statements to develop provision for meeting a wide range of need. Patterns of provision across the school are varied and the school has sought new ways of deploying learning support and the additional resources that having a high proportion of students designated as having special educational needs brings. The school has used these resources in innovative ways to support the learning of all students across the curriculum.

However, as the school becomes increasingly inclusive in some ways it becomes less so in others. There is a tension between who goes to the school, what the curriculum offers and how assessments are undertaken. During one observation of a Year 8 maths lesson, a student identified with severe learning difficulties sat at a table sewing numbers on sensory cards while other students worked on a probability problem. The LSA was seated with the student with the sewing cards and helped with behaviour management of all the students at the table. The classroom teacher did not interact with this student and the other students at the table largely ignored him. One girl said: 'Are you happy?' and patted him on the back. The LSA changed activities but the student did not engage with the task. This is contrasted with other observations discussed above where the teacher and

LSA (communicator) worked together in such a way that the observer was not aware there were two deaf students rather than one in the class. However, these students needed sign language interpretation, not differentiated lessons.

As noted in Table 8.1, the school reports a large number of students (24.8 per cent) as having special educational needs. There is some difficulty in establishing exactly what this means and there is a debate within the SMT about whether all students on the register of 'additional educational needs' should be counted. Should all who receive support be counted as having 'special educational needs'? And does such designation matter when it comes to achievement?

By using achievement as an outcome measure it can be shown that having a high proportion of students identified as having special educational needs does not have a negative impact on the achievement of children who do not have this designation. On the contrary, many staff in the school believe that the strategies used by the school for including students identified with special needs contribute to improved achievement for all. Though this claim has not been proved in this study, it is substantiated in part by the high achievement levels of the students in the school when measured as value added (see Table 8.4).

In a separate analysis of comprehensive secondary schools within the LA (Rouse and Florian, 2006), group means for three secondary schools where the proportion of students designated as having special educational needs was high (including Chester) were compared to schools where the proportion was low (comparison schools) and other schools in the LA. The mean progress in the case study schools was found to be higher than the mean progress in the comparison schools (see Table 8.2), but lower than the local authority average which included schools that did not have open admissions policies (see Table 8.3).

Table 8.1 Percentages of Year 11 students on selected variables in Chester school and the LA, 2004

School	Chester School (n=266)	LA (n=3,267)
Total % SEN	**24.8**	18.5
Gender	53.3 boys	47.8 boys
	45.1 girls	48.1 girls
% FSM eligibility	**38.7**	39.6
First language other than English	**75.6**	57.3
Ethnicity (above 5%)	**21.4 Pakistani**	19.4 White British
	20.3 Indian	15.5 Indian
	18.4 Bangladeshi	12.2 Pakistani
	9.4 Black African	11.8 Bangladeshi
	8.3 White British	9.1 Black African
		7.7 Black Caribbean
Stability (% students in school since Year 7)	79.7	79.9

NB: Figures in bold are statistically significant when compared to all schools in the authority. Not all percentages add to 100 because of missing data.

Table 8.2 Chester School and three comparison schools with lower percentages of students identified as having SEN, 2005

Selected variables	Chester School	Comparison schools with lower % SEN (average)
Number of students at the end of KS4	245	227
Number of KS4 students with SEN statements	17	7
Percentage of KS4 students with SEN statements	6.9%	3.0%
Number of KS4 students with SEN without statements	36	17
Percentage of KS4 students with SEN without statements	14.7%	7.23%
Percentage of students achieving Level 2 (5 or more grades A*–C)	45%	35%
Percentage of students achieving Level 1 (5 or more grades A*–G)	92%	90.3%
Percentage of students achieving at least one qualification	100%	96.66%
Average total point score per student	290.1	291

Table 8.3   Mean 2003 Year 11 achievement statistics for Chester School and the LA

LA	All students	Students not identified as SEN (n=2035)	SEN (n=413)
KS2 average pts	24.2	24.9	20.7
GCSECAP points	36.7	39.7	22.0

Chester	All students	Students not identified as SEN (n=168)	SEN (n=37)
KS2 average pts	24.2	25.1	20.1
GCSECAP points	30.3	33.5	15.6

Table 8.4   Value-added, 2005

KS2 to KS4 Value-dded	
KS2–KS4 value-added measure	1007.4
Percentage of students at the end of KS4 included in VA calculation	84%
Average number of qualifications (equiv. to GCSE) taken by KS2–KS4 VA students	8.6

KS3 to KS4 Value-dded	
KS3–KS4 value-added measure	1025.2
Percentage of students included in KS3–KS4 VA calculation	97%

In England secondary schools are judged by the percentage of students achieving a particular level (e.g. five passes at A*–C at GCSE). Comparing schools in this way sometimes results in the belief that the presence of students identified as having special educational needs will affect the results of students who are not so identified, but the performance of students at Chester does not substantiate this (see Tables 8.2, 8.3 and 8.4). Indeed when value-added measures are used it can be seen that Chester school does better than the national average.

Any investigation of the achievement of students depends on a set of outcome measures against which schools can be held accountable and decisions need to be made about what outcomes are important and how they will be assessed. As we have argued, the selection of these outcome measures enables different stories about the effects of inclusion on the education of all students to be told. Notably, the quality of students' social participation is an area of ongoing concern. The one disabled member of staff who herself had attended a mainstream school raised a number of issues about loneliness and friendship and listening to her voice may open up new opportunities for the further development of inclusive practice.

Finally there is an issue of what happens to students when they leave Chester. The majority of students go to local colleges, but a range of school staff expressed concern about the quality and range of available provision. There are a number of link schemes with local colleges but there is an awareness that more could be done to help support students as they move on to further education. Still, the story of Chester is a story of a responsive school. Across all of the interviews and documentation reviewed for this study there was a sense of continual review and development. Senior management is seen as committed to inclusion and staff are aware of the strengths and weaknesses of existing provision.

Part III

Learning from others: learning from ourselves

9 Learning from others

Achievement and inclusion across the case study schools

In this chapter we reflect on our work in this book as a whole to consider what we have learnt about the complex relationship between educational achievement and inclusion in schools. First, we go back to the ideas and debates discussed in part one so as to identify a number of emerging propositions regarding the nature of this relationship. We then take each in turn as a way of structuring our multiple case analysis across the four schools presented in Part II. Whilst this has required us to compare the schools, our intention has not been to create a hierarchy amongst them, but rather to acknowledge that each one has, quite properly, developed a range of different approaches in response to its own particular circumstances and needs. All four schools share certain characteristics, challenges and concerns and, at the same, each is distinct from the others. These similarities and differences between one school (or class, or child, or adult) and another have allowed us to explore the sometimes taken-for-granted policies and practices which shape the hourly, daily, weekly and yearly activities and behaviours of any school. Thus we recognise that schools are complex and dynamic organisations and acknowledge the great demands that this can make on staff and students.

Examining the relationship between achievement and inclusion through multiple case studies

In Chapter 3 we discussed our previous research regarding the quantitative analysis of students' achievements, as measured by their performance on national tests (Rouse and Florian, 2006). When we compared the results from three secondary schools which admitted high proportions of learners identified as having special educational needs with the results from all secondary schools in the same LA, we found that one of the three schools performed better than the LA average, one performed on a par and one was below the LA average. This evidence did not seem to support the view, therefore, that including high proportions of students designated as having special educational needs has a detrimental effect on the achievements of other students in a school. We suggested that further research was needed to examine in detail the 'stories' behind the numbers. Hence the four schools at the centre of this book and the multiple case study analysis in this chapter.

We have drawn on the work of Stake (2006) to support the methodological rationale underpinning this analysis. He stresses the importance of describing the overall phenomenon that is being investigated, and argues that 'complex meanings ... are understood differently because of the particular activity and contexts of each Case' (p.40). So, in our research, the overall phenomenon that is being investigated is the relationship between educational achievement and inclusion and the cases are the four schools. Our intention is not to seek broad generalisations across the schools but rather to gain a clearer knowledge of the whole by considering both commonalities between and variations amongst them. As Stake explains: 'Comprehension of the phenomenon ... requires knowing not only how it works or does not work in general, independent of local conditions, but how it works under various local conditions' (ibid.).

This approach has allowed us to examine and question our emerging propositions about the whole (achievement *and* inclusion) within the differing contexts of four cases (the schools). Simons (1996: 237) argues that case study methodology encourages us to 'challenge existing forms of knowing, through using different ways of seeing'. By working across a number of case studies, in the way we have described above, we hope to offer the possibility of a more nuanced understanding of the complex phenomena of educational achievement and inclusion, and the relationship between them, as experienced by students and staff in schools.

Five propositions regarding the relationship between achievement and inclusion

In Part I we drew on previous research, our own and others', to explore current understandings of achievement and inclusion and the relationship between them. We also considered the nature of the evidence and methodologies used to examine these concepts, arguing that different approaches can bring about different ways of understanding complex phenomena. A central aim of the book overall has been to further our understanding of schools which are able to be highly inclusive in terms of their student population whilst also constantly seeking to develop the achievements of *all* their students. We are particularly concerned about what can be learnt from studying such schools, which may then be helpful to those who work in and with other schools. To help us in this task we have synthesised the debates and ideas raised in Part I to identify five emerging propositions about the nature of the relationship between achievement and inclusion. We have then used these to structure our multiple case study analysis. They are as follows:

1   High levels of inclusion, in terms of a school's willingness to admit a diverse student population, can be compatible with high levels of students' achievements as measured by a school's overall progress in national standardised tests.
2   If schools are expected to achieve ever higher academic standards, some may resist pressures to become more inclusive because of concerns that doing so will lower students' overall standards.

3   Staff who work successfully within a system of high inclusion and high standards see their schools as diverse problem-solving organisations where policies and practices are dynamic rather than static. Different schools use different approaches to support inclusion and achievement so as to respond creatively to the circumstances and needs of their students.

4   Supporting achievement and inclusion is about being equitable towards all learners; it is not about denying differences between them.

5   All teaching and learning takes place within the context of human relation-ships, shaped by a school's culture and the values and beliefs of its members. Relationships – amongst students, amongst staff and between staff and students – are at the heart of understanding and developing policies and practices which support inclusion and achievement.

Of course, in the everyday working worlds of the four case study schools, examining each proposition separately is not straightforward: they are all influenced by and closely connected to each other. These complexities are apparent in the analysis we present in the remainder of the chapter. Nevertheless, using the propositions as our analytical structure has allowed us to reveal in detail different ways in which the schools have endeavoured to be as inclusive as possible whilst also attempting to raise the achievements of *all* their students. It has also provided us with a means by which we can consider the nature of the successes they have accomplished and the challenges they have encountered. Whilst we are interested in revealing differences and similarities between the schools, we are most particularly concerned with understanding why these are so.

Compatibility of high levels of inclusion and achievement in the schools

Proposition 1: High levels of inclusion, in terms of a school's willingness to admit a diverse student population, can be compatible with high levels of students' achievements as measured by a school's overall progress in national standardised tests.

In terms of student population, all four schools could be described as highly inclusive: they all had an open admissions policy and were part of an LA in which segregated provision in special schools had been minimised and where mainstream schools were expected to accommodate and take responsibility for the vast majority of children and young people living in their local communities. Certainly, all four schools accepted onto their rolls students who, in many other LAs, would be likely to be placed in special schools. Furthermore, none of the schools operated any form of selection: they were co-educational and non-faith based, although there were a number of single sex and faith schools in the LA.

There were, however, variations in the admissions policies and practices for each of the schools. Neither Kingsley nor Chester, unlike Amadeus and Harbour, were able to provide full physical access for students who are wheelchair users and so those living locally had to attend alternative schools. Meanwhile, spare capacity at the primary schools had resulted in the LA asking these schools to accept children from outside their catchment areas who had been permanently excluded elsewhere. Both headteachers argued that including children who were particularly troubled and troubling could upset the balance of their existing intake, especially as they considered the management of children's behaviour a priority in their schools.

Meanwhile, the secondary schools had 'resourced provision' for particular groups of students (those identified as having profound and multiple learning difficulties and also students with hearing impairments) who attended the schools from across the whole LA. Such practices arguably made the schools both more and less inclusive; *more*, because they accepted greater numbers of students with clearly identifiable educational needs, but *less*, because doing so may have disrupted the balance of their intakes overall. As one teacher noted, there was a danger of being perceived by local families as a 'special school' rather than an 'inclusive comprehensive'. Finally, imbalance also occurred because of the admissions policies and practices of *other* schools nearby: for example, the influence of two faith schools on student intake at Kingsley and the existence of faith and single-sex secondary schools in the LA.

Three of the four schools (Harbour being the exception) were high achieving schools in terms of students' measurable progress in Key Stage tests. These three schools had all received formal recognition regarding their students' achievements via Ofsted reports and/or the DfES. Both primary schools had significantly raised their tests results over a small number of years, although their approaches to doing so had been very different indeed. Students at Chester also generally made good progress as measured by Key Stage 4 GCSE/GNVQ results. Harbour offered a somewhat different picture as the progress of its students in national tests was relatively small. However, this did not seem to be directly related to the school's high levels of inclusion in terms of its student population. Rather, staff attributed this to low expectations held by students and their families and communities, although the causes cited, such as poverty, high mobility, poor health and disrupted families, were also prevalent in the other schools. What may have been important here too, then, was that some staff at Harbour also had depressed expectations about the students whom they taught, whereas a common characteristic of the other three schools was that staff expected their students to work hard and do well regardless of their home circumstances. Furthermore, they were generally confident about their abilities as teachers to help them to do so.

There were a few but significant exceptions to this. A number of teachers, particularly at Kingsley and at Chester, were less confident about their abilities to support the achievements of specific groups of children and young people. For example, at Kingsley, some staff were concerned about the limited progress being made by a child identified with profound and multiple learning difficulties. They considered her inclusion in mainstream classes as possibly excluding her from more rewarding opportunities to learn. At Chester, some staff were ambivalent about the experiences offered to deaf students, seeing them as being both inclusive and exclusive (part of a mainstream school but not 'belonging' in ways which might be possible in a specialist school for deaf students). Staff were also unsure about how far the provision at Chester promoted or constrained their academic achievements (being taught by qualified subject teachers but reliant on 'communicators' to access the curriculum). Indeed, similar tensions were evident in other alternative arrangements made specifically to support students identified as having special educational needs.

Reflecting on the proposition: Evidence from across the case studies suggests that high levels of inclusion, in terms of diversity of student intake, can be compatible with high levels of student achievement, as measured by a school's overall progress in national standardised tests. However, this relationship is not straightforward. To support both inclusion and achievement it seems important to maintain a balanced student intake, although this process is difficult for a school to manage by itself. Therefore greater collaboration between groups of schools and across an LA seems necessary to encourage all schools to take a shared responsibility for local children and young people. The principle of 'natural proportions' may be helpful here, but this concept may fit uneasily with the need to locate specialist forms of expertise and facilities in particular schools. Thus the notion of 'resourced provision' is paradoxical. It can be seen as both a means to promote inclusion but also as a form of 'internal exclusion' when the additional resources and facilities are only available to certain designated children and young people.

Developing and maintaining high levels of achievement within an inclusive setting can be realised in a range of ways in different schools but high expectations of students by staff as well as teachers' confidence in themselves as capable practitioners seem crucial. Even in schools which are inclusive in terms of student population and which achieve well overall in national tests, provision for certain groups of students may be more problematic, and less successful, than for others in terms of developing opportunities both to be included and to achieve. What is important here in terms of inclusion and achievement is the way in which school staff engage with that which becomes problematic. Rather than exclude, they search for ways to mediate the equity–excellence dilemma (Rouse and Florian, 1996).

Tensions in the schools between the principles of social justice and those of market-based reforms: concern that being more inclusive will lower standards

Proposition 2: If schools are expected to achieve ever higher academic standards, some may resist pressures to become more inclusive because of concerns that doing so will lower students' overall standards.

All four schools had inevitably been affected by the marketplace reforms that are part of current English educational legislation. They were all the subject of Ofsted inspections, their students participated in national tests and the results of these were published in publicly available performance tables. However, there was very little evidence that teachers, from any of the schools, perceived there to be any real conflict between governmental demands for ever higher academic standards and their own professional commitment to values of equity and social justice. As one teacher commented, you would not choose to work in this LA unless you agreed with the principle of inclusive education. Furthermore, staff across all four schools argued strongly that the inclusion of children and young people identified as having special educational needs did not have a negative impact on the achievements of other students, in terms of national standards or broader conceptualisations of achievement (although there were some exceptions to this).

Nevertheless, in three of the four schools (all but Amadeus), staff articulated a number of concerns regarding the impact of these different forms of accountability and, especially, the performance tables. They argued that schools identified as being 'lower achieving' had more difficulty in recruiting and retaining staff than those considered to be 'higher achieving', a problem exacerbated by the high cost of housing in this LA. They also argued that Key Stage test results influenced some families' choice of school, with those higher in the tables being more likely to attract a broader social mix of children from their locality (for example, faith schools that attract higher performing students). However, in Amadeus there appeared to be far less concern about these issues. The headteacher argued that the school's arts-based curriculum attracted teachers to join the staff, whilst the professional freedom it allowed them convinced them to stay. In addition, staff were perhaps less concerned about performance tables, in terms of parental choice of schools, since Amadeus was purpose built to serve a new housing estate and the vast majority of its children came from this clearly defined catchment area.

Our evidence also shows that three of the schools (again, not Amadeus) had put policies and practices into place with the specific intention of improving their ranking in local performance tables. In Chester, for example, decisions about who should and should not be included in the examination returns were partly influenced by their impact on the school's overall results. A thread running through the case study of Harbour is the opinion of many teachers regarding the inflated nature of children's Key Stage 2 results (at the end of the primary phase). Partly underlying this view was their concern about demonstrating progress in tests at Key Stages 3 and 4, as the outcome measures at any particular Key Stage become the benchmark measures for the next. If scores are inflated then the scope for demonstrating improvement is reduced.

It was in Kingsley, however, that the pressures exerted by the national tests could be most clearly identified. Many of the arrangements for teaching and learning (timetabling, grouping of children and allocation of staff) had been made with the explicit intention of improving Key Stage test results, and the evidence was that they had been highly successful. Staff were also able to identify a number of other positive effects arising from these changes. Thus, whilst it was possible to criticise the restricted curriculum as limiting broader notions of achievement and the emphasis on teaching in sets as reducing children's opportunities to learn together and being detrimental to the self-esteem of some, the headteacher argued that their higher ranking in performance tables had improved teachers' morale, recruitment and retention, raised both teachers' and children's expectations about their achievements, and encouraged more local families to send their children to the school. Therefore, it may be that this whole school response to pressures of accountability not only contributed to higher academic achievements but also supported notions of equity and social justice. Kingsley was no longer considered to be a failing school for failing children and families, but a place where very many children were able to succeed.

Meanwhile, in Amadeus, structures for teaching and learning had largely ignored the demands of Key Stage tests. The national curriculum was mainly taught through the creative arts, with a strong emphasis on music, drama and dance. Unlike Kingsley, children were not 'prepared' for the tests, nor was special provision made for those who were expected to achieve borderline marks, in an effort to boost their attainment levels. And yet, evidence also indicated that national tests results had improved significantly at this school too, reflecting the headteacher's stated belief that an arts-based curriculum improved children's academic achievements. Therefore, it was possible to argue that Amadeus, like Kingsley, had successfully mediated the pressures to raise children's academic achievements whilst maintaining its support for values based on equity and social justice: specifically here that access to the arts was a right for all children and not for a privileged few only.

As noted, staff from all schools argued strongly that including a diverse student population did not have a negative effect on students' learning generally or on academic standards overall. Indeed, there was full agreement across the schools that including students who in the past or in other LAs might have attended special schools was of benefit to other students. In particular, staff identified the importance of all students developing a greater awareness, tolerance and acceptance of children and young people, whatever their identified learning difficulties and/or disabilities. Other advantages for the broader student population were cited. For example, some teachers (from Amadeus and Chester) suggested that a more inclusive intake had encouraged them to think more creatively about their classroom practices and this had then enhanced the learning experiences of other children. Some teachers (from Amadeus, Chester and Kingsley) described how working with a range of children had developed their skills, expertise and confidence as teachers more generally. Staff at Chester also argued that having learning support assistants (LSAs) working in classrooms and attached to subject departments benefited the learning of all students and not just those to whom they were allocated because of their identified special educational needs. Such attitudes, however, were not shared by all. In Harbour, new teachers in particular sometimes seemed less confident about their skills and capabilities, rather than more, when working with classes which included students with a broad range of identified special needs.

Finally, some teachers in Kingsley and Amadeus maintained that including children whose behaviour was significantly troubled or troubling had, at times, had a negative impact on the learning of other children. This concern seemed to relate to both schools' expressed unwillingness to admit children who had been permanently excluded elsewhere. Two factors appeared to be involved here: one was to do with perceptions about a particular 'type' of learning difficulty and its impact on other children, and the other was to do with welcoming children who were, or were not, local. Thus those children who were seen as having behaviour difficulties *and* who lived outside the schools' catchment areas were perhaps less acceptable than similarly identified children who did live locally. This concerned the notion of balance as discussed in the first proposition.

Reflecting on the proposition: Evidence from across the case studies indicates that schools are affected by marketplace educational reforms, particularly their relative position in local performance tables. However, this does not necessarily lead to schools resisting pressures to become more inclusive. Staff in schools which include a diverse student population seem able to maintain a strong commitment to values of equity and social justice, whilst developing policies and practices intended to raise all students' achievements. Indeed, being inclusive in this way can bring benefits to a wide range of students, and not only those identified as having special educational needs. Such attitudes and understandings may well be most prevalent in LAs which have specifically encouraged mainstream schools to take responsibility for all students. However, even in these circumstances there may be some anxiety in some schools about the inclusion of children who are considered to have behavioural difficulties. Here again, our view is that this anxiety reflects a commitment to inclusion and achievement. Staff are not rejecting these students so much as worrying about how to include them.

The schools as problem-solving organisations using different approaches to respond creatively to the needs of their students

Proposition 3: Staff who work successfully within a system of high inclusion and high standards see their schools as diverse problem-solving organisations where policies and practices are dynamic rather than static. Different schools use different approaches to support inclusion and achievement so as to respond creatively to the circumstances and needs of their students.

Our evidence suggests that all four schools, although to varying degrees, were problem-solving organisations in which policies and practices were dynamic rather than static. At the primary schools there was an ongoing cycle of re-assessment, with supportive organisational structures in place to encourage staff at all levels to learn together in collaborative ways. Both schools also drew on a range of outside resources to support their professional development. The role of the headteachers seemed crucial here, in terms of encouraging staff to engage in this process of continual evaluation, development and re-evaluation. At Kingsley, for example, we observed policies and practices being reviewed with regards to children's attendance, classroom behaviour, systems of rewards, monitoring progress, and so forth. At Amadeus, teachers were encouraged to be experimental in their lessons and were expected to share with colleagues their learning from these experiences. Although approaches to teaching and learning were very different at these two schools, both sets of staff seemed to have a sense of optimism that their respective schools could really make a difference to most children's lives and therefore seemed determined to find ways continually to improve the opportunities they offered.

Both secondary schools also provided evidence of being problem-solving organisations. For example, in Harbour a fundamental review of the curriculum at Key Stage 3 was taking place. This was intended to develop a more relevant and appropriate curriculum for all students, as well as focusing on how access to learning could be supported for students whose language and communication skills currently acted as a barrier to their achievements. The school had also put in place an extensive school-based staff development programme to enhance teachers' skills and confidence in supporting the learning of a diverse range of students. In Chester, staff who were interviewed described themselves as reflective practitioners and the school as being highly responsive to students' changing needs. The social inclusion faculty, involving over fifty members of staff, provided a clear example of a structural but flexible approach to supporting students' inclusion and achievement across the whole school. Furthermore, the faculty was organised so as to be responsive to students' changing needs, including mechanisms that allowed provision across the school to be regularly monitored and reviewed. The school's learning support department had also been developed significantly over the last few years. For example, there had been concerns about the high turnover of LSAs but these were resolved by offering them better professional development opportunities and higher pay for those who gained nationally recognised qualifications. The department's growth had also been used innovatively as an opportunity to change its structural relationship with subject departments across the school. Many LSAs were now attached to particular subject areas, enabling them to provide flexible support across the curriculum rather than rigidly supporting one student only all day.

However, in all four schools there was also evidence that it was sometimes very demanding for staff to find creative responses to the teaching and learning of all children and young people. In the primary schools, some teachers occasionally talked with regret about their work with a particular child and in terms of their own failure. In the secondary schools, some of the more intractable problems that concerned staff were less about individual students and more about systemic difficulties. Some of these were considered to be largely beyond the school's control; for example, at Harbour staff were concerned about the negative effects of some students' family/home circumstances on their learning achievements. Other problems were perceived as being so complex that solutions were difficult to realise; for example, decisions about how best to manage 'resourced provision' for students. In Chester, for example, staff continually reflected on the nature of the provision offered to students who are deaf, and they held different views on how to find an organisational resolution that could be unambiguously inclusive for the students, both socially and academically.

Furthermore, at Harbour, it was possible to argue that the ways in which the 'resourced provision' was allocated in the school may have restricted opportunities for teaching staff to find creative solutions to support the learning of certain identified groups of students. That is, some teachers may have considered policies and practices intended to develop the inclusion and achievements of such students as being primarily the concern of specialist teachers and taking place within their designated base, rather than a shared responsibility held by all staff across the school, whereas the primary schools were organised so that every child, whatever their identified special need, was a member of a mainstream class and their class teacher was expected to take overall responsibility for supporting his/her learning, whatever additional help might have been available in the school.

Reflecting on the proposition: Evidence from across the case studies suggests that schools which aim to be increasingly supportive of the inclusion and the achievements of all their students are likely to be dynamic problem-solving organisations, in which all staff are continually encouraged to evaluate and develop the policies and practices they use. In such schools staff need to be flexible, creative, collaborative and confident professionals, able to respond quickly and appropriately to the learning needs of a diverse and often changing student population. The support and encouragement of headteachers, or other members of a school's management team, is crucial, providing teachers with valuable opportunities to try out new ideas, both within their own classrooms but also more widely across the school. Furthermore, headteachers are able to ensure that any developments become structural in nature so that they support the inclusion and achievements of as many students as possible.

Some schools find some problems easier to resolve than others and these differences are partly to do with the school itself and partly to do with the particular nature of the required changes. On the one hand it may be more straightforward to review policies and practices in ways that will bring about swift and appropriate changes in a primary school because their smaller scale and less complex organisation supports processes of communication and collaboration between staff. On the other hand the larger scale and more complex organisation of a secondary school can also be advantageous because it provides greater opportunity to use resources flexibly. Finally, a teacher in a primary school is usually expected to be responsible for all the children in his/her class and this may well encourage the development of more creative responses to teaching and learning, whereas in a secondary school the wider range of 'specialist' provision might allow subject teachers to abdicate responsibility for some children and thus reduce their sense of urgency and commitment to seeking more inclusive solutions to teaching and learning. However, policies and practices to support inclusion are not only dependent on the nature of learners' strengths, weaknesses and needs, but also on the human and material resources available to the school. Thus there can be no single best way to build inclusive practice.

Supporting the highest achievements of all students in the schools, whilst safeguarding the needs of the most vulnerable

Proposition 4: Supporting inclusion and achievement is about being equitable towards all learners; it is not about denying differences between them.

Not only did all four schools have policies and practices in place intended to raise the achievements of students generally, they had also all developed a range of other policies and practices specifically aimed at those individuals and groups of students whom staff had identified as needing additional support. There was a strong commitment amongst many staff in all of the schools to safeguarding the educational needs of children and young people who might be more vulnerable to processes of exclusion. At the same time, concerns were expressed about the level of available resourcing to ensure that such provision was adequate, both in terms of being sufficient for those students who received it and also being able to provide extra support to other students who might benefit from it. When giving additional resources to one class, group or individual in the schools, teachers worried about the equity of doing so relative to the learning and achievements of other classes, groups and individuals.

Underlying dilemmas raised in all the case studies included: how far the basic curriculum offered in the school could be made accessible to all students or whether some students would benefit from alternative curricula; how far students should be supported within their ordinary classrooms or taught in separate (possibly specialist) accommodation; whether some students required additional provision for all, some or none of the school day; whether providing alternative arrangements enhances or diminishes students' self-esteem and attitudes to learning. Underpinning these concerns was another important dilemma for the schools: which members of staff should have overall responsibility for supporting which students' achievements and inclusion. There were significant variations in the ways in which each school set about reconciling these concerns. Our evidence suggests that even within individual schools some forms of provision were more or less successful than others at supporting the learning of those students for whom they were intended. This was complicated further by the ambiguous nature of some of the practices we observed, which comprised elements which not only enhanced students' achievements and inclusion, but also simultaneously seemed to limit their opportunities to achieve and be included. Furthermore, the demands made on some schools seemed more complex than on others, both in terms of students' needs and organisational structures.

Amadeus, perhaps, offered the most straightforward approach in that the fundamental policy of the school was that all children should learn together in mixed attainment classes. First and foremost, each teacher was expected to use the arts-based curriculum as a means of making all lessons accessible to every child in their class. Implicit here was an understanding that the arts encouraged children to achieve in many different ways (creatively, socially and emotionally as well as academically) and this allowed learning to be an inclusive experience offering a greater range of possible outcomes and developments suitable for all children than more traditional forms of curricula. Second, all classes were supported by a TA who worked in classrooms alongside teachers. Even when TAs were assigned to support the learning of one or two particular children identified as having special educational needs, they were encouraged to work with a wider range of children whenever possible. Very occasionally, a small number of children were withdrawn from their classes to work separately from their peers; for example, to practise reading. This focus on making the curriculum accessible to all, for learning to take place within ordinary classrooms and for some in-class support to be available at all times, seemed to simplify decisions about how to allocate additional resources, in that funding was primarily used for TAs.

Like Amadeus, the other three schools had developed, or were developing, whole school arrangements intended to raise all students' achievements. However, unlike Amadeus, they also offered a number of other forms of provision aimed at supporting groups of students whose educational needs were considered more complex. In terms of whole school arrangements, all children at Kingsley participated in the curriculum with its sharp focus on core skills subjects. This was considered to be a key means of raising all children's achievements whilst also supporting the learning needs of those with the lowest attainments. Arranging children in teaching groups according to current attainment scores was also intended to support all children's learning, but with the 'lower' sets receiving more adult support because they comprised fewer children. Recent initiatives at Chester were also aimed at making learning more inclusive across the whole school, whilst maintaining a clear focus on supporting more vulnerable students. Examples include: the broad role and remit of the social inclusion faculty (including its work with students at risk of being permanently excluded); assessment procedures, involving target setting and student tracking across all subject departments for all students; the allocation of some TAs to departments rather than individual students only. Similarly, at Harbour, new Year 7 arrangements, designed to support all children's learning, had been implemented and senior teachers were working on the development of a more inclusive curriculum intended to increase access to learning to all students in Key Stage 3.

All four schools also provided a range of additional forms of support and many of these help to illustrate the dilemmas noted earlier in this section. For example, like Amadeus, the other schools made use of support staff working alongside subject and class teachers so as to help particular individuals and groups of students to learn in mainstream lessons. Sometimes, the role of support staff was to ensure that students were included in the class's activities, as in the case of 'communicators' working with deaf students at Chester. Sometimes, and unlike Amadeus, their role was to assist students to work on tasks which were different from those of their peers. For example, we observed LSAs and TAs working in this way at both Kingsley and Chester because the students they were supporting were considered unable to participate in the class's activities.

Kingsley, Chester and Harbour all had arrangements in place to withdraw students from lessons to participate in small group work, focusing on various types of identified learning needs. So, at Kingsley, such groups included speech and language, behaviour support and 'nurture' plus gifted and talented. Some groups provided short-term interventions intended to help particular children to continue to learn in their ordinary classes, such as the behaviour support group. Sometimes a group was formed to provide a longer-term solution to more intractable difficulties. Therefore, at Harbour, because so much of the current curriculum was inaccessible to students designated as having profound and multiple learning difficulties, they spent the majority of their time in lessons separated from other students. At Harbour and Chester the additional demands of the 'resourced provision' were particularly complex, and centred around whether certain groups of students would benefit most from being taught as a separate group or from being included in mainstream classes. Concerns about the learning opportunities offered to deaf students at Chester have been raised throughout this chapter and, in particular, how to support a student's right to be included in the 'hearing world' without then devaluing his/her membership of the 'deaf world'.

Reflecting on the proposition: Evidence from across the case studies suggests that schools which set out to support the highest achievements of all children and young people must also acknowledge differences between individual students so as to provide opportunities in which all are able to learn. There seem to be two principal ways that this can be accomplished. First, by putting into place whole school structures, and especially the overall curriculum framework, that promote inclusive learning by recognising different forms of achievements and acknowledging differing rates of students' progress. Second, by supporting this work with a range of additional provision intended to ensure that those students most vulnerable to processes of exclusion are fully included in mainstream activities. When overall structures are designed to be as inclusive as possible, then additional support will probably be more straightforward to arrange, although managing this in schools with more diverse student populations is likely to be more challenging. Helping to resolve this dilemma is probably related to the previous proposition: that is, when staff see their school as a problem-solving organisation and consider themselves to be confident professionals, they are more able to respond creatively to the circumstances and needs of all their students.

Relationships between members in the schools, and the values and beliefs that they hold, are at the heart of developing achievement and inclusion

Proposition 5: All teaching and learning takes place within the context of human relationships shaped by a school's culture and the values and beliefs of its members. Relationships – amongst students, amongst staff and between staff and students – are at the heart of understanding and developing policies and practices which support inclusion and achievement.

We observed many interactions between staff and students during our visits to the four schools and, in the overwhelming majority of them, the staff's behaviour towards students was respectful and caring. Similar attitudes were reflected in our interviews with staff, in which they discussed their commitment to values based on social justice and equity as well as their belief that all children and young people have the right to be included in their schools and to achieve whilst there. Staff in all schools (and at Kingsley and Amadeus in particular) talked about their schools in terms of being places that were able to make a significant difference to children's lives, although there were some teachers who spoke of the overwhelming negative impact of social/family circumstances on children's achievements. Where there was confidence that they could make a difference, the belief in their own professional competence and that of their colleagues clearly influenced their relationships with the children and encouraged high expectations of them as learners. Furthermore, we observed no instances, in any of the schools, of staff behaving in ways that stereotyped or were intolerant of others in terms of class, gender, ethnicity, religion or sexual orientation.

Our observations across all four schools also indicated that relationships amongst staff were generally based on values of mutual support and respect. Staff in the two primary schools, whatever their position in the schools' hierarchies, worked closely and productively with colleagues. This sense of joint commitment was somewhat weakened in the secondary schools, probably because the sheer size of these organisations encouraged staff to form smaller groups within each school, usually around subject departments. However, the divisions between some 'mainstream' and some 'resourced provision' staff ('schools within schools') seemed less productive in terms of supporting either the inclusion or the achievements of some of the most vulnerable students.

In interviews, staff from all four schools discussed the importance of encouraging positive relationships between all students. Feeling safe, not being bullied, was considered an essential foundation for learning to take place. More specifically, staff expected students to behave with the same respect to one another as they as adults showed to them and to each other. We observed numerous examples of children and young people taking time to 'look out' for students identified as having special educational needs, and attitudes were generally tolerant and accepting. However, staff in the secondary schools voiced concerns about the loneliness of some children and young people and the difficulties they had in terms of forming friendships.

Within the general principles noted above, other somewhat more ambiguous beliefs and attitudes were revealed. So whilst staff articulated the view that all children and young people were of equal worth and had the right to attend their schools, some also argued that a very small number of students might achieve more if they were taught in specialist settings. The arguments given were not that such children were not welcomed in their schools but, for their own sakes, they should go where they would benefit from better resources and greater staff expertise. Particular examples included: one child at Kingsley identified as having profound and multiple learning difficulties; students at Harbour, similarly identified, who were part of the school's 'resourced provision'; and a small number of children at both Kingsley and Amadeus whose behaviour was considered by staff to be exceptionally disruptive.

This is not to suggest that all staff at these schools shared these attitudes. Those staff who worked most closely with the students referred to above were likely to be more confident about supporting their learning. However, and perhaps more importantly, they had also formed relationships with the students, in which their own complex understandings of 'same' and 'other' had been challenged. Support staff, for example, from across the schools, described how their initial scepticism about working with some children and young people was gradually dispelled as they got to know the students as individuals and were able to recognise and value their particular achievements. These shifts in understanding were not likely to happen, however, when mainstream teachers did not engage with, or take responsibility for, the learning of some students in their classes; for example, the maths teacher at Chester did not seem to have any form of relationship with the student sewing number cards in his/her lesson.

The experiences of deaf students at Chester offer further insights into the nature of what staff, and students, believe about notions of 'sameness' and 'otherness' and the complex nature of developing positive relationships between members of a school. Although provision for deaf students was seen as good in that access to learning was provided through the support of 'communicators', there was concern about the nature of the relationships the students formed with subject teachers and their hearing peers. However, this was not to do with deaf students being accepted as the 'same' as hearing students, but rather to do with forming positive relationships which also recognised and valued their differences. Some staff argued that the deaf students were often isolated and lonely in the school and suggested that this would not have happened if they attended a specialist school where they would be the 'same' and not 'other'. Some of the deaf staff also suggested that a similar divide existed in the relationships between them and hearing staff and that they too felt isolated in the school.

Reflecting on the proposition: Evidence from across the case studies suggests that the nature of the relationships between staff and students, amongst staff and amongst students can be complex and challenging but it is also key to the successful development of policies and practices which support educational inclusion and achievement. Relationships are formed within the culture of a school and shaped by its values and beliefs. Thus, cultures must be nurtured in which all members are valued equally, whilst differences between them are acknowledged and celebrated. Staff must also believe that they are able to help all students to make progress: doing so requires a broader understanding of achievements as well as an acceptance of a shared responsibility for the learning of all students in their schools.

Examining the nature of relationships in these ways also underlines the interconnectedness of all five propositions. That is, in a school …

- which includes a diverse student population on its roll and also achieves highly in terms of national standardised tests (Proposition 1)
- that does not allow marketplace pressures to undermine its fundamental principles of social justice and equity (Proposition 2)

- where staff see themselves as creative professionals working in a dynamic problem-solving organisation (Proposition 3)
- all learners are supported to achieve highly but provision is made to safeguard the achievements of those most vulnerable to processes of exclusion (Proposition 4)

… then, the values and beliefs that shape the culture of that school and the nature of the relationships amongst its members seem most likely to support policies and practices which encourage both high levels of inclusion and achievement (Proposition 5). Thus, in a school where such values and beliefs are more deeply embedded in its culture, the first four propositions will also be more easily developed and sustained. Staff in all four schools experienced difficulties and tensions as they attempted to mediate the equity–excellence dilemma. We consider the anxiety and concerns that they articulated to be part of this constant process of mediation. These concerns may therefore be interpreted as evidence of their commitment to raising the achievements of all students, rather than as barriers to the inclusion of some.

10 Researching achievement and inclusion in your school

In the previous chapter we reflected on what we had learnt about the relationship between achievement and inclusion from our research across the four case study schools. The purpose of this final chapter is to provide ideas for practitioners who intend to research the nature of that relationship as it is experienced by students and colleagues in their own classrooms and schools. Although it is more than 30 years since Stenhouse (1975: 143) described practitioner research as being 'systematic, critical and self-critical enquiry which aims to contribute to the advancement of knowledge', we consider his definition to encapsulate the essential elements of such work. This chapter comprises a series of questions and suggestions to support practitioners to reflect on how they might collect and interpret evidence in ways which are 'systematic, critical and self-critical', so as to advance their knowledge about developing the achievements and the inclusion of children and young people with whom they work.

This chapter is not intended to provide 'quick fixes', but to promote greater understanding as a condition for bringing about sustainable change. As is clearly illustrated by our four case studies, not only is the relationship between these two concepts far too problematic for simplistic solutions, but schools and classrooms are complex worlds shaped by the diverse and shifting social, emotional and cultural lives of the staff and students who inhabit them. As Rose and Grosvenor (2001: 5) argue:

> Educational research can be concerned with improving our understanding of processes, practices and organisations associated with teaching and learning without requiring a rush to judgement, without needing to provide an answer. Educational researchers have a capacity and a responsibility to develop knowledge. This creative role can involve them in unsettling certainties, in being troublesome, in challenging the 'what works' philosophy and the single-vantage point, single-track mode of education.

That is, it is through the process of being unsettled and challenged, even sometimes troubled, that our own and others' assumptions about teaching and learning, and achievement and inclusion, may be most usefully revealed.

In the first half of the chapter we address three key concerns relating to this form of practitioner research. We begin by outlining ways practitioners can examine the different conceptual understandings of achievement and inclusion that are held by members in their workplaces. We next discuss the nature of research evidence and how decisions about what evidence to collect are partly shaped by conceptual understandings about what is useful and appropriate to the concerns of the research but also partly determined by pragmatic considerations regarding what is available to practitioners. We then address issues relating to the ethics of research, but with a particular emphasis on ensuring that the process of research is an inclusive one that draws its evidence from a wide range of members from across a school, as well as one which acknowledges and values a variety of different achievements by students. In the second half of the chapter we return to some of the ideas raised in Chapters 3 and 4 to consider how practitioners can make use of research evidence on educational achievement and inclusion that is readily available in their own schools. We discuss two ways in which practitioners can draw on existing quantitative data that are intended to monitor and measure students' achievements and inclusion: provision mapping and Pupil Achievement Tracker (PAT). We then describe how the *Framework for Participation* can be used to structure a variety of other research activities, including suggestions about interviews, observations and documentary sources. We expect readers to adapt, select from and add to any of the ideas presented in this chapter, so as to make them most appropriate to their own research contexts, interests and concerns.

Researching conceptual understandings of achievement and inclusion in a school

Since the focus of the research is educational achievement and inclusion, it seems necessary to consider how these concepts are understood by those who have a role to play in the research process, including:

- The researcher(s): *'What are our beliefs and understandings? How might these views shape our research intentions and interpretation of the findings?'*
- Staff and students (plus others) who provide direct research evidence, through interviews, observations, examination of policy documents and so forth: *'What are their beliefs and understandings? How might these views shape the nature of the evidence we gather?'*
- Staff and students (plus others) who may be affected by the findings of the research: *'What are their beliefs and understandings? How might these views shape any recommendations, based on our research findings, to develop policies and practices?'*

As we have discussed throughout the book, the concepts of achievement and inclusion, and other associated ideas, are complex and problematic, and are understood differently by different people working in education. Therefore, when practitioners research these concerns in their own schools they cannot presume that their views and understandings are shared with other members. The questions above are important because they encourage assumptions to be examined and ambiguities to be revealed across and within the three groups. These differences need to be explored, not in an attempt to resolve them, but to recognise that they exist and to consider what their implications might be for any research undertaken. Even two practitioners working together closely on a joint research project are unlikely to share entirely the same conceptual understandings. Indeed, as the three authors of this book, we have come to appreciate how each of us has our own particular beliefs about and understandings of achievement and inclusion. We consider these variations to be a strength of our research, encouraging us to challenge one another's thinking and allowing us to make our own distinct contributions to the book.

To support researchers to engage in this process of conceptual exploration in their own schools we have returned to the key questions raised in the first chapter of the book. We have selected and adapted some of these original questions which practitioners can then use in a range of different ways, modifying and adding some questions if required (see Boxes 10.1, 10.2 and 10.3). For example, this could be a basis for:

- reflection by the researcher (substituting 'you' for 'I'), challenging their own beliefs, before embarking on research
- informing a preliminary discussion amongst co-researchers, establishing shared and different understandings
- an interview or questionnaire schedule, for individuals and/or groups, gathering their own views and also their perceptions of others' understandings
- examining school policy documents, scrutinising them in terms of whose achievements and inclusion they support and/or limit, and in what ways.

Finally, the findings from such activities can provide two main forms of information by:

- revealing shared and different understandings of the concepts of educational achievements and inclusion and their inter-relationship
- identifying particular strengths and/or limitations in policies and practices relating to achievement and inclusion.

Together these provide a foundation on which a more detailed research focus can be established.

Paying attention to the nature of research evidence

Different research concerns and interests require different types of evidence and therefore researchers have to make choices about what kinds of information they do, and do not, collect. In addition to evidence that is gathered for specific

Box 10.1   Examining understandings of achievement in a school

1 What do you understand by educational achievement?
   • Academic; social; emotional; creative; physical.
2 What do you think different members of this school/class/group etc. understand by educational achievement?
3 Do you think some forms of achievement are more important than others?
   • If so which ones? Why?
4 Do you think different members of this school/class/group etc. value certain forms of achievement more highly than others?
   • If so which forms of achievements? Why?
5 What do you consider to be the relationship between achievement and the following ideas?
   • Ability; aptitude; attainment; performance; standards; progress.
6 To what extent do you think the achievements of children and young people in this school are influenced by the following factors?
   • The student him/herself; the classroom (plus role of practitioners), whole school, families and local communities; national concerns.

Box 10.2   Examining understandings of inclusion in a school

1 What do you understand by educational inclusion?
2 What do you think other members of this school/class/group etc. understand by educational inclusion?
3 Do you think it is more acceptable to include some children and young people rather than others in this school/class/group etc.?
   • If so, who would you include? And, who not? Why?
4 Do you think different members of this school/class/group etc. consider it to be more acceptable to include certain children and young people rather than others?
   • If so, who might they include? And, who not? Why?
5 What do you consider to be the relationship between inclusion and the following ideas?
   • Exclusion; integration; participation; special educational needs; disability.
6 To what extent do you think the inclusion of children and young people in this school is influenced by the following factors?
   • The student him/herself; the classroom (plus role of practitioners), whole school, families and local communities; national concerns.

Box 10.3 Examining understandings of the relationship between achievement and inclusion in a school

---

1 What changes do you think could be made in this school to raise the achievement of its children and young people?
   - What do you think might be the effects of doing this on the inclusion of ... individual students; identified groups of students; classes; the whole school?
2 What changes do you think could be made in this school to develop the inclusion of its children and young people?
   - What do you think might be the effects of doing this on the achievements of ... some individual students; identified groups of students; classes; the whole school?
3 In what ways do you think assumptions in this school about the 'normal distribution' of ability influence our policy and practice relating to inclusion and achievement?
4 What changes do you think could be made in this school to ensure high levels of achievement as well as high levels of inclusion so that *all* students can participate fully in education?

---

research activities, many schools already have other ongoing arrangements in place for collecting evidence, which are intended to support broader decision-making about school and classroom policies and practices. These are often part of a school's development, or improvement, plan; they may also be used to support the completion of the SEF (Self Evaluation Form) required by Ofsted inspectors (Ofsted, 2005c). Considerations about the nature of evidence also concern the unit or level of analysis of the research activity. For instance, practitioners may choose to focus on the achievements and inclusion of an identified group of children and young people or more broadly across the student population; they may also wish to consider staff (teachers and/or support staff) and parents/ carers. The research may be set within a single classroom, curriculum area, year group or Key Stage phase, across a whole school or a number of schools in a local authority.

A pragmatic approach is to start by looking at what evidence is currently available: for example, others' research (whether university or practitioner based); government publications, advice and legislation; large-scale national datasets. Particularly relevant for practitioners whose research focuses on developing a greater understanding of students' achievements and inclusion is to consider evidence that has already been collected in their own schools. For example, and as we discussed in Chapter 3, schools in England maintain records of students' key stage test scores: comparing individuals, progress across time, progress across year groups, other schools and so forth. Many also collect other forms of quantitative data, such as performance on reading and spelling tests, or measurements based on notions of general ability, such as Cognitive Attainment Tests (CATs). They also have detailed documentation about students who have been identified as having special educational needs, such as individual education plans (IEPs), reports from external agencies, etc. However, Swaffield (2003: 39) makes an interesting distinction between schools being rich in data whilst poor in information. That is to argue, just because large amounts of data are easily available does not necessarily make them useful and informative for practitioners.

Furthermore, an over-reliance on some of the types of quantitative evidence noted above may restrict the outcomes of practitioner research, because the analysis of such evidence may promote a narrower view of both achievement and inclusion. That is, achievement may be reduced to performance scores in core curriculum subjects, say, thus disregarding achievements relating to other areas of the curriculum and aspects of children's lives. Similarly, inclusion may be restricted to focusing on the perceived learning difficulties of a small number of individual children, rather than looking more broadly at the contexts in which all teaching and learning takes place. Therefore the emphasis must be on gathering evidence which is appropriate to the research focus and useful to the researcher.

Another consideration is how far the evidence which practitioners need to collect for other purposes can be used to support their own research activities. For example, as noted above, all schools in England are expected to complete a Self Evaluation Form (SEF) in preparation for when they are formally inspected by Ofsted. The guidance given on completing the SEF includes: 'It should be an accurate diagnostic document with *all conclusions fully supported by the evidence*' (our emphasis). In another document entitled *Writing a SEF that Works*, similar advice is given with specific reference to the *Every Child Matters* agenda: 'You need to be conscious of it throughout your evaluation. Think about what difference your provision has made and how do you know ... you should make sharp judgements and *find factual evidence* to support them' (our emphasis).

This emphasis on collecting evidence for Ofsted can be supportive of practitioner research. For example, three major sections on the SEF concern the following questions, all of which can be directed towards providing worthwhile evidence relating to students' achievement and inclusion:

- 'What are the views of learners, parents/carers and other stakeholders and how do you know?' (Ofsted, SEF, section 2)
- 'How well do learners achieve?' (section 3)
- 'How good is the overall personal development and well-being of the learners?' (section 4)

All three of these sections can usefully draw on a range of different forms of evidence gathered by a variety of methods.

Finally, decisions about research evidence are likely to be shaped by practitioners' perceptions of what they do and do not already know about the focus of their research. Practitioners are knowledgeable about their schools in ways that 'outsider' researchers can rarely be (for example, when we visited the four case study schools) and this provides a firm basis from which to gather new evidence. This knowledge includes information about the systems and structures in the school as well as its historical, social and cultural contexts. At the same time, there are difficulties associated with being an 'insider' researcher; familiarity can also be over-familiarity, making Stenhouse's (1975) aspiration for 'self-critical' enquiry particularly challenging. Practitioners also have what McIntyre (2005) refers to as 'craft knowledge', which he describes as 'the tacit, schematic, intuitive thinking on which classroom teaching depends' (p.364). However, this suggests such knowledge, although highly valuable, is not easily accessible as evidence for others.

Box 10.4 provides a series of questions which practitioners can use to think about the nature of the research evidence they might gather to examine achievement and inclusion in their schools. As in with Boxes 10.1, 10.2 and 10.3 some of these

Box 10.4   Paying attention to the nature of the research evidence

---

1 What counts as research evidence?
   - How do different conceptual understandings of achievement affect decisions about the nature of research evidence?
   - How do different conceptual understandings of inclusion affect decisions about the nature of research evidence?
   - Are some types of research evidence more valuable/useful than others? If so, which? Why? And, for whom?
2 What is the nature of research evidence based on …
   - professional experiences and practitioner 'craft' knowledge?
   - practitioner research?
   - university research?
   - large-scale national datasets?
   - government publications, advice and legislation?
3 How is achievement assessed, evaluated, monitored and recorded in this school?
   - For what purposes?
   - Who are its audience?
   - What are the strengths and limitations of these different ways …
   - for individual children and young people?
   - in teaching groups/classes?
   - across the school?
4 How is inclusion assessed, evaluated, monitored and recorded in this school?
   - For what purposes?
   - Who are its audience?
   - What are the strengths and limitations of these different ways…
   - for individual children and young people?
   - in teaching groups/classes?
   - across the school?

questions are an adaptation of those first raised in Chapter 1, others draw on the discussion above.

Box 10.5 sets out some rather more pragmatic questions intended to support the process of gathering research evidence. A more detailed discussion of suggestions for how this might be undertaken is given in later sections of this chapter on using quantitative datasets and on the *Framework for Participation*.

Considering the ethics of learning from others when researching achievement and inclusion

Ethical considerations are central to every stage of the research process, regardless of the nature and focus of the particular research activity being undertaken. Various professional organisations provide useful advice on ethics, as do the majority of general research methods text books. These cover important issues, including those relating to notions of consent, confidentiality, rights and protection from harm. The British Educational Research Association (BERA, 2004), for example, has produced an extremely helpful set of ethical guidelines. Their recently revised version takes into account the particular ethical concerns of the increasing numbers of practitioners who are choosing to engage in research in their own schools.

Box 10.5   Existing knowledge, knowing and not knowing

---

1. What existing evidence do I have about the research topic/focus?
2. What other evidence do I need to strengthen my research?
3. What sources of evidence are already available in this school?

Drawing on some of the following:

Existing evidence in school
- records of students' achievements (end of key stage test scores, etc.)
- records of some students vulnerable to processes of exclusion (IEPs, statements of special educational needs, figures for exclusions and unauthorised absence, etc.)
- Self Evaluation Form (Ofsted)
- school development/improvement plans
- other documents (policies, teaching materials, etc.)

Learning from myself
- own past professional experiences and 'craft' knowledge

Learning from others
- past professional experiences and 'craft' knowledge of staff in this school
- listening to students, staff, parent/carers, etc.
- observing individuals, groups, classes, etc.
- other research by practitioners, academics, government, etc.
- comparative evidence from national datasets.

Our focus here is on practitioners who undertake educational research into the nature of the relationship between achievement and inclusion. We consider it to be essential that the methods used are integral to the ethical principles underpinning the research itself (Booth and Ainscow, 1998). That is, the process as well as the subject of the research should be inclusive: valuing the experiences and taking account of the views of different members from across a school. It should also acknowledge and value a range of students' achievements. These points are important for two main reasons. First, the process of the research should not marginalise, or exclude, the very members of a school on whom it is focused, whether students, teachers and support staff or parents/carers. Furthermore, there should be no assumption that views are shared within these groups. For example, the notion of 'student voice' is a popular one in current educational debates but we would suggest that an exploration of 'student *voices*' is a more fitting approach. Careful consideration of different perspectives properly challenges a researcher to reflect on his/her own viewpoints and their influence on the research. Thus, a commitment to social justice and equity is not only about *what* you research but also about *how* and 'reflexivity, openness, collaboration and consultation are all key features' (Griffiths, 1998: 109). Second, the complexity of the substantive concerns requires a broad understanding of the issues involved and, as we have illustrated in our case studies, different members of schools hold different values and beliefs which then influence the ways in which policies are interpreted and practices are implemented. Listening, for example, to the accounts of children and young people or support staff, can offer an important counterbalance to the views of others such as teachers, or alternative evidence to that provided by large-scale datasets.

Practitioners have certain advantages over other researchers, such as those working in universities, in terms of engaging in these forms of research: in particular, they have easier access to members of their school and over a longer period of time. For example, when we collected evidence for our case studies it was not always easy for us to interview students, as their teachers were, rightly, concerned about gaining consent from parent/carers and also about removing students from lessons. These difficulties are more easily addressed by teachers as consulting with children and young people is part of their everyday work. It is also more straightforward for teachers to gather such evidence on a number of different occasions, perhaps to check for clarity of meaning or to evaluate the effects of, and attitudes towards, the implementation of a particular new practice.

In this chapter we have already discussed some of the difficulties relating to being an 'insider' researcher; however, there are also specific ethical issues to take into account. The hierarchical structure of any school presents particular challenges to practitioners when researching with and on behalf of colleagues and other members of a school's community. Concerns about position/role, status, power and authority are especially significant in research which sets out to examine the nature of relationships and the different values and beliefs that members hold about achievement and inclusion. Exploring the views of a headteacher is likely to require a different approach to that which sets out to examine those held by a parent, a teacher, a teaching assistant or a child. And, if the researcher in each of these examples is, say, a newly qualified teacher, a special educational needs co-ordinator or a deputy headteacher then this too will have an effect on the research process.

Furthermore, and as we discussed at the end of the previous chapter, researchers need to consider how teaching and learning take place within the context of human relationships and, therefore, how research which focuses on issues of achievement and failure, inclusion and exclusion has the potential to unsettle emotionally those who participate in it. Being trustworthy, respectful and sensitive towards others are crucial characteristics of any researcher, but they are especially pertinent for practitioners who are researching students and colleagues in their own workplace and, even more so, if the subject of that research concerns issues that go to the heart of people's deeply held values and beliefs. Thus, if a member of a school feels threatened or is made anxious, then the research is neither inclusive nor ethical.

Box 10.6 provides a series of questions which practitioners can use to think about ethical concerns relating to learning from others in their own school when researching achievement and inclusion.

Box 10.6   Considering the ethics of learning from others when researching achievement and inclusion

---

1   Is the methodological approach integral to the ethical principles under-pinning the subject of the research?
  * How inclusive is the research process?
  * Does it take account of the views and value the experiences of a wide range of members?
  * Does it acknowledge different understandings of what counts as achievement and recognise the worth of a variety of students' achievements?
  * Does it marginalise or exclude any individuals or groups from aspects of the research?
2   Whose views and experiences are needed to ensure that a range of understandings are gathered?
  * Children and young people?
  * Teachers and support staff?
  * Parents/carers and others?
  * And, how can the research methods ensure that a range of voices are heard from within these groups?
3   What procedures have been put into place to make certain that students and staff will not be harmed by the research?
  * How will issues relating to power differentials between the researcher and those s/he is researching be addressed?
  * How can a researcher explore students' and colleagues' values and beliefs without causing members to feel anxious or threatened?
  * How can a researcher develop trust, respect and sensitivity towards all those involved?

Examining quantitative data to research students' achievements and inclusion

This section should be read in conjunction with Chapter 3, which comprises a detailed discussion of the advantages and limitations of using largescale datasets to provide research evidence about educational achievements and inclusion. In England and elsewhere, schools collect more data than ever, and whilst technology has made them much easier to manage and analyse, there are serious questions about the validity and reliability of the information that is gathered. Nevertheless, if handled with care these data can provide information that may enable schools to make evidence-informed judgements about the progress and achievements of students in the context of the deployment of human and material resources.

In England, there is a growing trend in schools to undertake provision mapping, as a means of providing details about interventions or other forms of support used with particular students. Many local authorities have guidance on provision mapping which suggests that it can be used as part of the decision making and planning process in order to:

- audit how well provision matches need and identify gaps in provision;
- highlight repetitive or ineffective use of resources;
- establish success criteria for the school's 'special educational needs' policy;
- report on the success of the 'special educational needs' policy;
- inform parents, the LA, external agencies and Ofsted about how resources are being used;
- focus attention on whole-school issues of learning and teaching rather than on issues relating to individual children and young people;
- record changes in provision; and
- provide information that can be transferred from class to class or school to school.

Various aspects of provision might be included in the 'map' such as:

- *Who?* (e.g. assistants, teachers, peer support)
- *Where?* (e.g. in class, withdrawal, special placement, etc.)
- *What for?* (literacy or other curriculum area, social or behavioural)
- *How?* (the nature of the intervention)
- *When and for how long?* (e.g. one hour ever day for a term)
- *Success criteria?* (how would we know whether the extra help/intervention has made a difference?)
- *Cost?*

Cost should be considered in terms of not only the financial implications of making such additional provision, but also the emotional and social costs to the child. In addition there will also be the so-called 'opportunity costs'. In other words what would the adults be doing if they were not making this provision, and most importantly, what, if anything, is the student missing in order to receive this provision?

The process of provision mapping can help inform decisions about the allocation of resources and the success, or otherwise, of an intervention. Provision mapping can be seen as an important element of the 'waves of support' as described in the Primary National Strategy (DfES, 2003c), which identifies three 'waves' of support. These are consistent with the graduated approach to meeting children's needs as set out in the *SEN Code of Practice*.

- Wave 1 would take place as part of a whole class experience. The more successful Wave 1, the less likely the need for …
- Wave 2, which consists of small group intervention for children who are expected to 'catch up'. And if this does not work the …
- Wave 3 support would be provided to those students who 'fall behind their classmates and have individualised targeted support programmes' (DfES, 2003c) put into place. Students working at Wave 3 would be expected to have an individual support plan such as an individual education plan, care plan, or behaviour support plan.

An essential element of 'waves of support' therefore is the notion of 'catching up'. The problems involved in using such notions, which are based on simplistic comparisons, have been considered elsewhere in this book. Nevertheless, it is important to remember that progress and achievement have to be conceptualised more broadly than this. Some children will be making progress and will be achieving, but they will not 'catch up' with other children, nor will they 'catch up' with their chronological age.

In a more sophisticated attempt to look at how progress can be demonstrated over time, the DfES has brought some co-ordination to the content and format of data management and analysis at national level through the introduction and further development of the Pupil Achievement Tracker (PAT) software. This is available to all schools and local authorities. The PAT can plot:

- pupil progress over time
- pupil progress in relation to others
- pupil progress in relation to the median of the cohort
- pupil progress in relation to the national median and upper and lower quartiles.

It can also be used to plot the progress of individuals over time. In other words it enables progress to be personally referenced. According to the London Regional Partnership Framework for Inclusive Education, it can be used systematically and creatively to support the development of inclusive cultures and practice and raise achievement at all levels. When used thoughtfully, bearing in mind all the caveats outlined earlier in this book, new data handling software such as PAT can help teachers, curriculum areas and schools to manage data so that questions about inclusion and achievement can be addressed, not only at the institutional level, but also at the level of the individual student.

Using the *Framework for Participation* to research achievement and inclusion in schools

This section should be read in conjunction with Chapter 4, in which the conceptual rationale underpinning the construction of the *Framework for Participation* is considered. We used this *Framework* to structure the collection of our evidence in the case studies. Here we discuss its practical application as a methodological lens through which practitioners can examine the relationship between achievement and inclusion in their own schools. The *Framework* is intended to support the types of research that we have already addressed in this chapter by:

- acknowledging that different members of a school will have a range of understandings about the concepts of achievement and inclusion;
- paying attention to the nature of the research evidence so as to (i) take account of the complex educational experiences of individuals and groups of students and staff, in classrooms and schools, and (ii) make use of evidence which is accessible to practitioners and is useful to their work;
- ensuring that the methods used are integral to the ethical principles underpinning the research;
- recognising that researching achievement and inclusion in schools requires a careful examination of human relationships amongst and between students and staff.

The *Framework* is set out in three broad sections relating to the notion of participation, which is seen as crucial to the development of both achievement and inclusion in schools. The sections are: participation and access: being there; participation and collaboration: learning together; and participation and diversity: recognition and acceptance. These are then sub-divided into a number of key related elements (see Box 10.7).

Any section, or any element within one, can be taken as a starting point in terms of establishing a research focus. Practitioners may also choose to identify current areas of concern or particular policies and practices that they intend to develop. For example, these may relate to issues arising out of the school development or improvement plan, or from aspects of the SEF (Ofsted's Self Evaluation Form). The focus of the research may be sharpened further by decisions about who to research: whether particular individuals, groups, classes, curriculum areas, key stages and so forth. Chapter 4 also provides a series of questions relating to the sections and elements in terms of the 'Who?', 'What?' and 'Why?' of participation. The questions are summarised here, but for full details see Chapter 4, Boxes 4.4 and 4.5.

Box 10.7   Sections and their elements in the *Framework for Participation*

PARTICIPATION AND ACCESS: BEING THERE
- *Joining the school*
- *Staying in the school*
- *Access to spaces and places*
- *Access to the curriculum*

PARTICIPATION AND COLLABORATION: LEARNING TOGETHER
- *Learning alongside other students*
- *Supporting students to learn together*
- *Members of staff working together*
- *Schools and other institutions working together*

PARTICIPATION AND DIVERSITY: RECOGNITION AND ACCEPTANCE
- *Recognition and acceptance of students, by staff*
- *Recognition and acceptance of staff, by staff*
- *Recognition and acceptance of students, by students*

- WHO does and does not participate? And, WHO decides this?
- WHAT are the policies, practices and interactions that promote participation in the school? And, WHAT are the policies, practices and interactions that strengthen barriers to participation?
- WHY do these processes of participation exist within the cultures (values and beliefs) of the school? And, WHY do these barriers to participation exist within the cultures (values and beliefs) of the school?

These questions can be asked at different stages of the research process and in a variety of ways. For example, they can support researchers to begin to explore participation – achievement and inclusion – in their workplaces. They may also form a basis for interviews and observations as well as for scrutinising school documents and classroom materials. In addition, the questions have within them a broad indication of the forms of evidence which might be used to address them: namely, the policies, practices and everyday interactions that shape experiences in a school, plus the values and beliefs that underlie them.

Box 10.8 builds on the *Framework*'s three sections, their main elements and these questions to provide detailed suggestions about research evidence that is likely to be readily available to practitioners in schools. This is then divided into interviews, observations and documentation although, of course, there are other types of research methods which practitioners may wish to use. The information provided here is intended to be developed in ways which suit different practitioners' particular research concerns, interests and resources. So, for example, if the research focused on 'creating and maintaining a welcoming and safe school' (as part of 'access to spaces and places') in addition to the suggestions given in

PARTICIPATION AND ACCESS: BEING THERE

Joining the school

- Admissions policies and practices
  - – Admissions policy **(D)**
  - – Practices and attitudes to admissions of a range of students **(I)**
  - – Other local (competing) schools admissions policy documents **(D)**
  - – Information on which schools local students attend and why **(I)**
  - – Local and national policies on student admissions **(D)**

Staying in the school

- Exclusion policies and practices
  - – Exclusion policy: fixed term and permanent **(D)**
  - – Exclusion figures over x years: fixed term and permanent **(D)**
  - – Policy on internal exclusions **(D)**
  - – Stories about exclusion practices, plus attitudes of staff and students **(I + O)**
- Student attendance policies and practices
  - – Attendance policy **(D)**
  - – Practices to support students' attendance, particularly those 'at risk' **(I)**
  - – Stories behind students' truancy and attendance **(I)**
  - – Policies on 'alternative curriculum' (on roll but out of school? full time/part time?) **(D)**
  - – Stories behind 'on roll but out of school' **(I)**

Access to spaces and places

- Physical accessibility policies and practices
  - – For students **(D + O + I)**
  - – For staff **(D + O + I)**
  - – For parents/carers and other visitors **(D + O + I)**
  - – Attitudes towards increasing physical access for members of the school **(I)**
- Creating and maintaining a welcoming and safe school
  - – Induction policies and practices for new students **(D + I)**
  - – Induction policies and practices for new staff (teaching/non-teaching) **(D + I)**
  - – Anti-bullying policies **(D)**
  - – Practices to help bullies and their victims **(I)**
  - – Stories of bullying **(I)**
  - – Welcoming and safe or frightening places: for whom, why and when? **(O + I)**
  - – Practices and attitudes about rules, rewards and sanctions **(I + O)**

(continued …)

Box 10.8 continued

- Open or out-of-bounds places: for whom, why and when? **(O + I)**
- Policies around rules, rewards and sanctions **(D)**

Access to the curriculum
- Timetabling policies and practices
  - The school's timetable and associated policies **(D)**
  - History and pragmatic reasons underpinning the timetable **(I)**
  - Practices: which groups of students do and do not do which subjects **(I)**
  - Practices: students' withdrawal from mainstream classes **(O + I)**
  - Practices affecting individual students' timetable and why **(I)**
  - Practices affecting individual teachers' timetable and why **(I)**
  - Policies: student withdrawal from mainstream classes **(D)**
- Access to the wider curriculum
  - Policies: lunchtime and after school clubs/activities **(D)**
  - Practice: lunchtime and after school clubs/activities, including who does and does not attend and why **(O + I)**
  - Policies: outside school trips and visits **(D)**
  - Practices: outside school trips and visits, including who does and does not attend and why **(O + I)**

PARTICIPATION AND COLLABORATION: LEARNING TOGETHER
Learning alongside other students
- Policies and practices which determine which students do and do not learn alongside one another
  - Selection criteria used to arrange students into teaching groups – e.g. gender; age; attainment; (dis)ability – to reduce or increase diversity **(D + I)**
  - election criteria used to arrange students into pastoral groups – e.g. gender; age; attainment; (dis)ability – to reduce or increase diversity **(D + I)**
  - Teachers' and students' expectations about students' achievements **(I)**
  - To what extent lessons comprise learning tasks which are appropriate to the full range of students in the class **(O + I)**

Supporting students to learn together
- Classroom practices which encourage students to use each other as a resource for learning
  - Teachers draw on students' existing knowledge, experiences, expertise and interests **(O)**

(continued …)

Box 10.8 continued

– Teaching styles support collaborative learning: e.g. group work; peer teaching; older students working with younger ones **(O)**
– Support staff work with range of students, not just individuals **(O + I)**

Members of staff working together
• Teaching staff work together to support their classroom practices
  – Team teaching, observing peers, sharing materials, etc. **(I + O + D)**
  – Drawing on existing knowledge, experiences, expertise and interests of other teachers **(I + O)**
• Teaching and support staff work together
  – Policies re in-class support: e.g. whole school and/or individual students **(D)**
  – Practices re in-class support: LSAs and teachers working together: planning lessons, preparing materials, working with some/all students, supporting behaviour, etc. (uses and abuses of LSAs) **(O + I)**
  – Practices of other support staff and teachers working together (language support, behaviour support, physiotherapy, etc.) **(O + I + D)**
  – Staff attendance at meetings (e.g. support staff included?) **(D + O + I)**

Schools and other institutions working together
• Collaborations across institutions: policies and practices: widening the range of resources available, both material and human
  – Other primary/secondary schools **(D + I)**
  – Primary–secondary school liaison **(D + I)**
  – Mainstream/specialist provision liaison **(D + I)**
  – Use of LA resources **(D + I)**
  – Other institutions? FE, HE? **(D + I)**

PARTICIPATION AND DIVERSITY: RECOGNITION AND ACCEPTANCE
Of the three key sections which comprise the *Framework for Participation*, this final one is, in some ways, the most problematic in terms of researching and understanding what is happening in a school. However, whilst its processes of participation and barriers to participation are not easy to reveal they cannot be ignored. They comprise the values and beliefs which help to underpin the cultures of a school. Because they are often covert and unquestioned by staff and students, they permeate all policies and practices, including those considered elsewhere in the *Framework*. In others ways these interconnections may, however, actually support the research in that

(continued …)

it may be possible to explore this key area of participation through the evidence gathered for the other two. Thus, any and all of the methods suggested elsewhere in the *Framework* (in terms of documentation **(D)**, interviews **(I)** and observations **(O)**) will also be appropriate here.

Recognition and acceptance of students, by staff
* The attitudes of staff towards students as a body
* Policies and practices that acknowledge, appreciate and celebrate the diversity of students and those in which differences are overlooked, misunderstood or treated with intolerance (gender, social class, ethnicity, academic attainment, classroom behaviours, (dis)ability, etc.)

Recognition and acceptance of staff, by staff
* Attitudes of members of staff towards colleagues according to institutional structures, hierarchies and statuses (e.g. class teachers and LSAs, SMT and classroom teachers, etc.)
* Attitudes of members of staff towards colleagues who experience difficulties in classrooms; providing support and/or shame and blame
* Policies and practices that acknowledge, appreciate and celebrate the diversity of staff and those in which differences are overlooked, misunderstood or treated with intolerance (gender, social class, ethnicity, academic attainment, classroom behaviours, (dis)ability, etc.)

Recognition and acceptance of students, by students
* Attitudes of students towards other individual students and groups based on sameness and diversity (gender, social class, ethnicity, academic attainment, classroom behaviours, (dis)ability, etc.), including friendships and bullying.

Box 10.8, practitioners might also ask students to record, by taking photographs or using a video camera, those places and spaces in their school where they do, and do not, feel safe.

The *Framework* is designed to be used flexibly by researchers. As noted, it provided the methodological basis for the four case studies in this book and practitioners might choose to take a part of it (sections or elements) to form a small-scale case study in their own schools. Moreover, it also allows the collection of evidence to be highly focused and to be built up over an extended period of time. The *Framework* does not specify precisely how interviews should be undertaken or precisely which aspects of school life might be observed, as this will be dependent on other research considerations. Nevertheless, our experiences of using the *Framework* suggest that asking members of a school to provide narrative accounts can be particularly revealing of underlying values and beliefs; for example, a teacher telling a story about why a child has been excluded, or a teaching assistant describing a lesson in which s/he worked really well with a teacher, or a student relating what s/he does at lunchtimes. Similarly, our experiences of observations indicate that not only lessons, but also staffrooms, assemblies, playgrounds, canteens and staff meetings can provide real opportunities to explore how far policies are put into practice, as well as the nature of the relationships between members of a school.

Final reflection

Throughout this book we have endeavoured to articulate the complex nature of educational achievement and inclusion and the relationship between them. Our case studies have shown how different schools respond to the demands of being as inclusive as possible whilst also aiming to raise the achievements of all their students. We found that while each school responded differently, all four schools shared values that encouraged high levels of both achievement and inclusion. Notably, staff in all of the schools rejected the conventional belief that including children who experience difficulties in learning may have a negative effect on the achievement of other students. In so doing they have set out to develop a culture in which all children can learn, and those who experience difficulties in learning are not seen as threats to the achievements of others. In this chapter we outlined how practitioners wishing to undertake research on achievement and inclusion can focus on concerns that matter to them and to the students and colleagues with whom they work. We hope that this book will provide support and encouragement in these endeavours.

References

Ainscow, M. (1991) *Effective Schools for All?* London: David Fulton.

Ainscow, M., Booth, T. and Dyson, A. (2004) Standards and inclusive education: schools squaring the circle. Paper presented at the 5th Annual Conference of the Teaching and Learning Research Programme, Cardiff, November 2004.

Apple, M. (2006) *Educating the Right Way* (2nd edition, first published 2001). London: Routledge.

Audit Commission (1992) *Getting in on the Act.* London: HMSO.

Audit Commission (2002) *Special Educational Needs: A Mainstream Issue.* London: HMSO.

Ballard, K. (1995) Inclusion in practice: a case study of methatheory and action. Paper presented at the symposium of Inclusion and Exclusion, Cambridge University, July 1995.

Benton, T. (2003) Measuring schools' value-added performance: the importance of picking the right outcome. Paper presented at the British Educational Research Association Annual Conference, Heriot-Watt University, Edinburgh, 11–13 September 2003.

BERA (British Educational Research Association) (2004) *Revised Ethical Guidelines.* Edinburgh: British Educational Research Association.

Black-Hawkins, K. (2002) *Understanding School Cultures: Developing Participation.* Unpublished doctoral thesis: The Open University.

Blair, M. and Bourne, J. with Coffin, C., Creese, A. and Kenner, C. (1998) *Making the Difference: Teaching and Learning Strategies in Successful Multi-ethnic Schools.* DfEE Research Report 59, London: HMSO.

Blyth, E. and Milner, J. (1997) Black boys excluded from school: race or masculinity issues? *In:* E. Blyth and J. Milner (eds) *Exclusion from School: Inter-professional Issues for Policy and Practice.* London: Routledge.

Booth, T. (1997) Stories of exclusion: natural and unnatural. *In:* E. Blyth and J. Milner (eds) *Exclusion from School: Inter-professional Issues for Policy and Practice.* London: Routledge.

Booth, T. (2002) Inclusion and exclusion in the city: concepts and contexts. *In:* P. Potts and T. Booth (eds) *Inclusion in the City.* London: Routledge.

Booth, T. and Ainscow, M. (1998) *From Them to Us: An International Study of Inclusion in Education.* London: Routledge.

Booth, T. and Smith, R. (2002) Sustaining inclusive education development: learning about barriers and resources in a London borough. Revision of paper presented at the British Educational Research Association Annual Conference, University of Exeter, 12–14 September 2002.

Booth, T., Ainscow, M., Black-Hawkins, K., Vaughan, M. and Shaw, L. (2000) *The Index for Inclusion: Developing Learning and Participation in Schools*. Bristol: CSIE.

Clark, C., Dyson, A., Millward, A. and Robson, S. (1999) Theories of inclusion, theories of schools: deconstructing and reconstructing the inclusive school. *British Educational Research Journal*, 25(2), 157–77.

Copeland, I. C. (2003) Integration versus segregation: the early struggle. *In:* M. Nind, J. Rix, K. Sheehy and K. Simmons (eds) *Inclusive Education: Diverse Perspectives*. London: David Fulton.

Corbett, J. (1999) Inclusive education and school culture. *International Journal of Inclusive Education*, 3(1), 53–61.

Davis, P. and Florian, L. (2004) Teaching strategies and approaches for children with special educational needs. A scoping study (Research Report 516), London: DfES.

DES (1978) *The Education of Handicapped Children* (The Warnock Report). London: HMSO.

Dessent, T. (1987) *Making the Ordinary School Special*. Lewes: The Falmer Press.

DfEE (1992) *Choice and Diversity: A New Framework for Schools*. London: HMSO.

DfEE (1997) *Excellence For All Children: Meeting Special Educational Needs*. London: HMSO.

DfEE (1999) *Social Inclusion: Pupil Support*. London: HMSO.

DfEE (2000) *Careers Education in the New Curriculum*. Nottingham: DfEE.

DfEE (2001) *Schools (Raising Standards, Promoting Diversity, Achieving Results): Building on Success*. London: The Stationery Office.

DfES (2001a) *Special Educational Needs and Disability Act (SENDA)*. London: HMSO.

DfES (2001b) *Special Educational Needs Code of Practice*. London: DfES.

DfES (2001c) *Inclusive Schooling: Children with Special Educational Needs*. London: DfES.

DfES (2003a) *Every Child Matters: Change for Children in Schools*. Nottingham: DfES.

DfES (2003b) *Data Collection by Type of Special Educational Need*. London: DfES.

DfES (2003c) *Excellence and Enjoyment, A Primary Strategy for Schools*. London: DfES.

DfES (2004a) *Every Child Matters: Change for Children*. Nottingham: DfES.

DfES (2004b) *Removing Barriers to Achievement: the Government's Strategy for SEN*. Nottingham: HMSO.

DfES (2005a) *Higher Standards, Better Schools For All: More Choice for Parents and Pupils*. London: HMSO.

DfES (2005b) *Leading on Inclusion*. London: DfES.

DfES (2006) http://www.teachernet.gov.uk/docbank/index.cfm?id=6084.

Dyson, A., Farrell, P., Polat, F., Hutcheson, G. and Gallannaugh, F. (2004) *Inclusion and Student Achievement* (Research Report RR578). Nottingham: DfES.

Emanuelsson, I. (1998) Closing reflections. *In:* P. Haug and J. Tøssebro (eds) *Theoretical Perspectives on Special Education*. Kristiansand: HøyskoleForlaget (Norwegian Academic Press).

Fielding, M. (1998) Community, philosophy and education policy: why effective policies won't work. Paper presented at the Annual Conference of the British Educational Research Association, Queen's University, Belfast, August 1998.

Fielding, M. (1999) Communities of learners. Myth: schools are communities. *In:* B. O'Hagan (ed.) *Modern Educational Myths*. London: Kogan Page.

Fielding, M. (2000) The person-centred school. *Forum*, 42(2), 51–4.

Florian, L. (2007) Reimagining special education. *In:* L. Florian (ed.) *The Sage Handbook of Special Education*. London: Sage Publications.

Florian, L. and Rouse, M. (2001) Inclusive practice in English secondary schools: lessons learned. *Cambridge Journal of Education*, 31(3), 399–412.

Florian, L., Rouse, M., Black-Hawkins, K. and Jull, S. (2004) What can national data sets tell us about inclusion and pupil achievement? *British Journal of Special Education*, 31(3), 115–21.

Gillborn, D. and Youdell, D. (2000) *Rationing Education: Policy, Practice, Reform and Equity*. Buckingham: Open University Press.

Gould, S. J. (1996) *Life's Grandeur: the Spread of Excellence from Plato to Darwin*. London: Jonathan Cape.

Griffiths, M. (1998) *Educational Research for Social Justice: Getting Off the Fence*. Buckingham: Open University.

Harlen, W. and Crick, R. D. (2002) A systematic review of the impact of summative assessment and tests on students' motivation and learning (EPPI Centre Review). *In: Research Evidence in Education Library*, Issue 1. London: EPPI Centre, Social Science Research Unit, Institute of Education.

Harris, A. and Ranson, S. (2005) The contradictions of education policy: disadvantage and achievement. *British Educational Research Journal*, 31(5), 571–88.

Hart, S. (1996) *Beyond Special Needs: Enhancing Children's Learning Through Innovative Thinking*. London: Paul Chapman.

Hart, S., Dixon, A., Drummond M. J. and McIntyre, D. (2004) *Learning Without Limits*. Maidenhead: Open University Press.

Hayden, C. (1997) *Children Excluded from School: Debates, Evidence, Responses*. Buckingham: Open University Press.

Hopkins, D., Black-Hawkins, K., Aldrige, K., Lay, H., Jewell. P. and Davidson, D. (1997) Report from the United Kingdom. *In*: D. Stern and G. Huber (eds) *Active Learning for Students and Teachers*. Frankfurt: Peter Lang/OECD.

House of Commons, Education and Skills Committee (2006) *Special Educational Needs, Third Report of Session 2005–06*, Volume I (HC 478–I). London: HMSO.

James, M. (2006) The Teaching and Learning Research Programme, www.tlrp.org.

London Regional Partnership Framework for Inclusive Education (2004) Data Profiling Project. http://www.londonrp.org.ok/rpts_pubs/reportsandpubs_index.asp

Lunt, I. and Evans, J. (1994) Dilemmas in special educational needs: some effects of local management of schools. *In:* S. Riddell and S. Brown (eds) *Special Needs and Policies in the 1990s*. London: Routledge.

Lunt, I. and Norwich, B. (1999) *Can Effective Schools be Inclusive Schools?* London: Institute of Education, University of London.

McIntyre, D. (2005) Bridging the gap between research and practice. *Cambridge Journal of Education*, 35(3), 357–82.

McLaughlin, M., Dyson, A., Nagle, K., Thurlow, M., Rouse, M., Hardman, M., Norwich, B., Burke, P. and Perlin, M. (2006) Cross-cultural perspectives on the classification of children with disabilities. Part II: implementing classification systems in schools. *The Journal of Special Education*, 40(1), 46–58.

Macmurray, J. (1938) *The Clue to History*. London: Student Christian Movement Press.

Macmurray, J. (1950) *Conditions of Freedom*. London: Faber.

Malmgren, K. W., McLaughlin, M. J. and Nolet, V. (2005) Accounting for the performance of students with disabilities on statewide assessments. *The Journal of Special Education*, 39(2), 86–96.

Marks, J. (2000) *The Betrayed Generation: Standards in British Schools 1950–2000*. London: Centre for Policy Studies.

Minow, M. (1990) *Making All the Difference: Inclusion, Exclusion and American Law.* Ithaca: Cornell University Press.

Mittler, P. (1999) *Working Towards Inclusive Education: Social Contexts.* London: David Fulton Publishers.

Norwich, B. (1997) *A Trend Towards Inclusion: Statistics on Special School Placements and Students with Statements in Ordinary Schools.* Bristol: Centre for Studies in Inclusive Education.

Odom, S. L., Brantlinger, E., Gersten, R., Horner, R. H., Thompson, B. and Harris, K. R. (2005) Research in special education: scientific methods and evidence-based practices. *Exceptional Children*, 71, 137–48.

OECD (2005) *Students with Disabilities, Learning Difficulties and Disadvantages – Statistics And Indicators.* Paris: OECD.

Ofsted (2004) *Special Educational Needs And Disability: Towards Inclusive Schools.* London: Ofsted.

Ofsted (2005a) *Annual Performance Assessment of [name withheld] Education And Children's Social Care Services.* London: Ofsted.

Ofsted (2005b) *Every Child Matters: Framework for the Inspection of Children's Services.* London: Ofsted.

Ofsted (2005c) *Every Child Matters: Framework for the Inspection of Schools in England from September 2005.* London: Ofsted.

Ofsted (2006) *Inclusion: Does it Matter Where Students are Taught? Provision and Outcomes in Different Settings for Students with Learning Difficulties and Disabilities.* London: Ofsted.

O'Hanlon, C. (2000) The emotionally competent school: a step towards school improvement and raising standards. *Management in Education*, 14(2), 51–4.

Oliver, M. (1990) *The Politics of Disablement.* Basingstoke: Macmillan.

Parsons, C. (1996) *Exclusions from School: the Public Cost.* London: Commission for Racial Equality.

Power, S. and Whitty, G. (1999) Market forces and school cultures. *In:* J. Prosser (ed.) *School Culture.* London: Paul Chapman.

QCA/DfES (2001) *Planning, Teaching and Assessing the Curriculum for Students with Learning Difficulties: General Guidelines.* QCA.

Reay, D. and Wiliam, D. (1999) 'I'll be a nothing': structure, agency and the construction of identity through assessment. *British Educational Research Journal*, 25(3), 343–54.

Riddell, S. (1992) *Gender and the Politics of the Curriculum.* London: Routledge.

Riehl, C. (2000) The principal's role in creating inclusive schools for diverse students: a review of normative, empirical and critical literature on the practice of educational administration. *Review of Educational Research*, 70(1), 55–81.

Rose, R. and Grosvenor, I. (eds) (2001) *Doing Research in Special Education: Ideas into Practice*, London: David Fulton.

Rouse, M. and Florian, L. (1996) Effective inclusive schools: a study in two countries. *Cambridge Journal of Education*, 26(1), 71–85.

Rouse, M. and Florian, L. (1997) Inclusive education in the marketplace. *International Journal of Inclusive Education*, 1(4), 323–36.

Rouse, M. and Florian, L. (2006) Inclusion and achievement: student achievement in secondary schools with higher and lower proportions of pupils designated as having special educational needs. *International Journal of Inclusive Education*, 10(6), 481–94.

Rouse, M. and McLaughlin, M. J. (2007) Changing perspectives of special educational needs in the evolving context of educational reform. *In:* L. Florian (ed.) *The Sage Handbook of Special Education*, London: Sage Publications, pp. 85–103.

Rouse, M., Shriner, J. and Danielson, L. (2000) National assessment and special education in the United States and England and Wales. *In:* M. McLaughlin and M. Rouse (eds) *Special Education and School Reform in Britain and the United States.* London and New York: Routledge.

Rustemier, S. and Vaughn, M. (2005) *Segregation Trends – LEAs in England 2002–2004. Placement of Pupils with Statements in Special Schools and Other Segregated Settings.* Bristol: Centre for Studies in Inclusive Education.

Sebba, J. and Ainscow, M. (1996) International developments in inclusive schooling: mapping the issues. *Cambridge Journal of Education*, 26(1), 5–18.

Sebba, J. with Sachdev, D. (1997) *What Works in Inclusive Education?* Ilford: Barnardo's.

Simons, H. (1996) The paradox of case study. *Cambridge Journal of Education*, 26(2), 225–40.

Siraj-Blatchford, I. (ed.) (1993) *Race, Gender and the Education of Teachers*. Buckingham: Open University Press.

Slee, R. (2005) Education and the politics of recognition: inclusive education – an Australian snapshot. *In:* D. Mitchell (ed.) *Contextualizing Inclusive Education, Evaluating Old and New International Perspectives*. London: Routledge.

Southworth, G. (1994) The learning school. *In:* P. Ribbens and E. Burridge (eds) *Improving Education: Promoting Quality in Schools*. London: Cassell.

Stake, R. E. (2006) *Multiple Case Study Analysis*. London: The Guildford Press.

Stenhouse, L. (1975) *An Introduction to Curriculum Research and Development*. London: Heinemann.

Stirling, M. (1992) How many children are being excluded? *British Journal of Special Education*, 19(4), 128–30.

Stoll, L. (1991) School effectiveness in action: supporting growth in schools and classrooms. *In:* M. Ainscow (ed.) *Effective Schools for All*. London: David Fulton Publishers.

Stoll, L. (1999) School culture: black hole or fertile garden for school improvement? *In:* J. Prosser (ed.) *School Culture*. London: Paul Chapman.

Sutton Trust (2006) *The Social Composition Of Top Comprehensive Schools – Rates Of Eligibility For Free School Meals At The 200 Highest Performing Comprehensives.* London: The Sutton Trust.

Swaffield, S. (2003) Assessment: servant or dictator? *Forum*, 45(2), 39–43.

Swann, W. (1988) Integration? Look twice at the statistics. *British Journal of Special Education*, 15(3), 102.

Thomas, G., Walker, D. and Webb, J. (1998) *The Making of the Inclusive School*. London: Routledge.

Thrupp, M. and Tomlinson, S. (2005) Education policy, social justice and 'complex hope'. *British Educational Research Journal*, 31(5), 549–56.

Tomlinson, S. (1982) *A Sociology of Special Education*. London: Routledge and Kegan Paul.

Whitty, G. (1997) School autonomy and parental choice: consumer rights versus citizen rights in education policy in Britain. *In:* D. Bridges (ed.) *Education, Autonomy and Democratic Citizenship: Philosophy in a Changing World*. London: Routledge.

Index

achievement: and academic standards
21–4; broader concepts of 25–6, 140;
and comparative data 23–4, 37–9,
68–70, 93–4; concepts of 3, 21–31;
and monitoring students 24–5; and
participation 46–7, 50; and progress
21–3, 39–40, 146–7; teachers'
attitudes towards 64, 66, 80, 133,
138; and value-added 22–3; *see also*
achievement and inclusion
achievement and inclusion: and
accountability and standards 8–9; and
arts curriculum 82–3; and behaviour
71; concept of 21, 30; and marketplace
reforms 10–11, 123–6; measuring the
relationship between 40–2, 140–1,
145–7; relationship between 6, 9–10,
15, 28–31, 40, 46–9, 99–100, 120–1;
relationship between evidence and 6,
136–7, 139; schools with high levels of
both 29–30, 121–31
accountability 8–12, 23, 27–8, 32, 33, 35,
38, 112, 124–5
Ainscow, M. 18, 19, 20, 21, 143
Apple, M. 7, 25
arts-based curriculum 72–85, 124–5,
129–30
ASDAN 105
attendance 2–3, 61, 74, 102
Audit Commission 15, 18, 28, 45

Ballard, K. 47
behaviour 61–3, 66–7, 71, 74–5, 94, 97,
99, 102, 122, 126
Benton, T. 23
BERA (British Educational Research
Association) 142
Black-Hawkins, K. 30, 46
Blair, M. 47

Blyth, E. 18, 47
Booth, T. 19, 20, 21, 46, 47, 48, 143
British Sign Language (BSL) 60, 66, 103,
104, 109–10

choice 7, 10, 23, 124
Clark, C. 50
Code of Practice 34, 36–7, 92, 146;
'school action' 33, 40, 92
comparisons: of schools 23–4, 28–30, 34,
41, 93–4, 99, 113–14; of students 3,
23–4, 34, 36–9, 40, 146–7
competition 7, 10–11, 23
Copeland, J. 8
collaboration: schools 66, 79, 123; schools
and other professional organisations 66,
79, 98–9, 123; staff 65, 78–79, 104–5,
128; students 48, 64–5, 76–78, 92,
104–5, 107, 126
Corbett, J. 48

Davis, P. 18
deaf learners 101–15, 123, 127–8, 130,
131, 133
Dessent, T. 17
disabilities: provision for 8, 9, 11, 16–17,
73–4, 80, 82, 103; understandings of
17, 19, 125
Disability Discrimination Act (2005) 11
diversity: responses to 21, 29–30, 47–8,
50–2, 66–8, 79–82, 92, 108–11, 122–3,
129–31
Dyson, A. 9, 28, 29, 40, 43

Education (Butler) Act (1944) 5
Education Act (1970) 7–8
Education Act (1981) 17, 18
Education Act (1986 Number 2) 18
Education for All 2

Emanuelsson, I. 21
English education system 3–8, 11, 17–20, 23–6
EPPI 32, 38
ethics 142–4
Every Child Matters 11, 12, 16–17, 25–7, 28, 140
evidence: nature of 38–9, 135, 137–43; use of 5, 39–41, 52–3, 140–2, 144–7, 149–52
evidence based practice 29, 32
Excellence for All children 17, 19
exclusion: concept of 8, 18–20, 40; evidence on 39, 42; as removal from classrooms and schools 61, 73–4, 88, 101–2, 112, 129

Fielding, M. 49
Florian, L. 8, 10, 11, 18, 28, 29, 30, 34, 35, 36, 40, 45, 46, 113, 119, 123
Framework for Participation 12, 45–53, 56, 147–153
free school meals 42
funding 95, 79, 95, 103, 112, 130

GCSE 7, 23, 29, 37, 39, 41, 99, 104–9, 122
Gillborn, D. 18, 25, 47
GNVQ 37, 39, 41, 99, 122
Gould, S. J. 31
Griffiths, M. 143
Grosvenor, I. 135

Harlen, A. 38
Harris, A. 7
Hart, S. 47, 48
Hayden, C. 18
Hopkins, D. 48
House of Commons Select Committee 10, 11

inclusion: attitudes of students towards 107, 132–3; attitudes of teachers towards 66–7, 70–1, 87, 90–1, 103, 108–9, 111–12, 131–3, 138; concept of 4, 7–8, 17–21, 87; and exclusion 18–9; government perspectives on 15, 19–20; and integration 16–7; measures of 9, 40–1, 43, 70–1; as process of school improvement 20–1, 103; social 20, 101–3, 112, 127, 130; and special educational needs 17–8; *see also* achievement and inclusion
Inclusive Schooling 9, 11
Index for Inclusion 21

integration 16–7, 60, *see also* segregation

James, M. 25

Leading on Inclusion, 32, 43
league tables 7, 11, 23–4, 25, 29, 63, 69, 75, 123–6, *see also* performance tables
learning difficulties: identification of 8, 18, 21, 126; nature of 17; profound and multiple (complex) 60, 86–9, 92, 105, 112, 122, 132–3; provision for 68, 73, 76, 80, 82
learning support assistants (LSAs): *see* teaching assistants (TAs)
local authorities (LAs): inclusion policies and practices 17–18, 29, 33, 34–5, 56–7, 60, 66, 73, 79, 91, 95–9, 105, 108, 121–3
Lunt, I. 18, 28, 29

McIntyre, D. 141
McLaughlin, M. 9, 35
Macmurray, J. 49
Malmgren, K. W. 32
marketplace reforms 7, 10–11, 20, 123–6, 134
Marks, J. 6
Milner, J. 18, 47
Minow, M. 20
Mittler, P. 45

National Performance Framework 23, 33
Norwich, B. 18, 28, 29
NPD (national pupil database) 29, 32–44

O'Hanlon, C. 31
Odom, S. L. 32
Ofsted 9, 11, 26–8, 35–6, 40, 56, 122, 123, 139–40
Oliver, M. 47

PANDA (Pupil and Assessment Data) 23
parents and carers: attitudes to inclusion 73, 82, 92; choice of schools 7, 9, 63, 125; involvement in practitioner research 139, 142, 143; supported by schools 61, 67, 72, 74, 99
Parsons, C, 18
participation 20–1; definition of 46–9
PAT (Pupil Achievement Tracker) 136, 146–7
performance tables 7, 23, *see also* league tables

PIVATS (Performance Indicators for Value Added Target Setting) 91
PLASC (Pupil Level Annual School Census) 23–4, 29, 32, 35, 37, 39, 40–3
Power, S. 10
practitioner research: achievement and inclusion and 136–40; ethics of 142–4; understandings of 135; using the *Framework of Participation* for 147–53
professional development 66, 67, 79, 96–7, 104, 126–7
provision mapping 103, 136, 145–7
P-scales 24–5, 37–8

Ranson, S. 7
Reay, D. 25
relationships in schools 30–1, 49, 66–8, 79–82, 94–5, 108–11, 131–4; impact on practitioner research 143–4
Removing Barriers to Achievement 11
resourced provision 56, 86, 87, 89–92, 94–7, 99, 122–3, 127–8, 131–3
Riddell, S. 47
Riehl, C. 47
Rose, R. 135
Rouse, M. 9, 10, 11, 28, 29, 38, 40, 113, 119, 123
Rustemier, S. 18

SATs (Standard Assessment Tests) 10–11, 37–9; impact of 25, 63–4, 68–9, 70, 77, 83–5, 96, 100, 121–6
Sebba, J. 17, 18, 19, 48
school culture: problem solving organisations and 126–9; relationship to achievement and inclusion 30–1, 60–2, 68, 83, 90, 121, 131–4, 151–2; relationship to deaf culture 109–10
SEF (Self-Evaluation Form) 27, 139–40, 147
segregation 8, 17, 99, 121, *see also* integration
selection 2, 4–7, 29, 121
SENDA (Special Educational Needs and Disability Act, 2001) 9, 11, 40
Simons, H. 120
Siraj-Blatchford, I. 47
Slee, R. 19, 40

Smith, R. 20
social inclusion: *see* inclusion
socio-economic status 42
Southworth, G. 48
Special Educational Needs Code of Practice: *see Code of Practice*
special educational needs: categorisation of students by 35–7, 40, 43, 70, 89; and inclusion 17–18, 40–1, 43; rates of identification of 17–18, 34–5, 42–3; statements of 33, 87; understandings of 17, 19–21, 33, 34–5, 41, 48, 89, 92, 113
special educational needs co-ordinator (SENCO) 65, 76, 88, 90–1, 95, 104–5
Special Educational Regional Partnerships 34, 146
Stake, R. E. 120
standards based reform 8–9, 10, 21–4, 28–9, 32
Stenhouse, L. 135, 141
Stirling, M. 18, 19
Stoll, L. 12, 30
student voice 107, 143
Swaffield, S. 140
Swann, W. 17

teaching assistants (TAs): attitudes to inclusion 61, 63, 67, 110; involvement in practitioner research 143,152–3; role of 65, 66, 77–8, 104–5, 107, 112, 125, 127, 130, 140
Thomas, G. 17, 47, 48
Thrupp, M. 7
Tomlinson, S. 7, 18

United Nations 2

value-added 11, 22–4, 29, 38, 51, 100, 113–15
Vaughn, M. 18

Warnock Report 17
well-being 16, 25–8
Whitty, G. 7, 10
Wiliam, D. 25

Youdell, D. 18